SOUTH '

CU00660915

MEXICAN

COOK BOOK

By Lucy M. Garza

Art Work By Bill Braswell

EAKIN PRESS Fort Worth, Texas

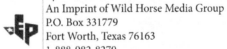

DEDICATION

This book is dedicated with deep affection to the person who inspired me, Rafaela Cavazos de Montalvo, my beloved mother.

Special thanks go to my patient and supportive husband, Paul, and children, Karla, Michael, John, and James, whose prayers helped and encouraged me to put South Texas Mexican Cook Book into print.

ABOUT THE AUTHOR

Lucy M. Garza, a school teacher in Falfurrias High School for more than ten years, is a professionally trained home economics instructor. But her background for compiling this delightful *South Texas Mexican Cookbook* goes past her years at Texas A & I University at nearby Kingsville where she received a bachelor of science degree in home economics, a masters degree in administration, and her Superintendent's certification. She attributes her love of cooking and homemaking and her skill in the kitchen to her mother, Rafaela Cavazos de Montalvo.

Today Mrs. Garza makes her home in Falfurrias with her husband, Paul, and her four children, Karla, Michael, John, and James and is employed by the Brooks County Independent School District.

The author grew up in Santa Monica, a small community, located in the Rio Grande Valley. She attended East Central High School in San Antonio, and later moved back to her home near Lyford where she graduated from high school in 1963. After receiving her degree she taught in Hebbronville Junior High school before joining the faculty of Falfurrias High School where she teaches home economics.

She is a member of Phi Delta Kappa, the Vocational Homemaking Teachers Association of Texas and the Texas State Teachers Association. In high school she has served as faculty advisor for the Future Homemakers of America. Young Homemakers of Texas, Home Economics Advisory Board, Brooks County Youth Booster Club, and is presently the head of the Home Economics department.

TABLE OF CONTENTS

Carne De Res (Beef)

Comidas De Gastronomo (Gourmet Foods)

Huevos Y Aves (Eggs and Poultry)

Panes (Breads)

Postres (Desserts)

Puerco (Pork)

INTRODUCTION

This book is a product of inspiration unknowingly instilled in me by my mother. Mama's favorite room was the kitchen — her *cocina*. I recall vividly my childish sense of well-being, the warm atmosphere and the spicy aromas that filled her domain and overflowed throughout the house.

At age six apron strings were extended and away to school I went, the most exciting event in a child's life. I loved school and dared not miss a day for fear of losing out on something. *La Jarita*, a country school, located in the small community of *Santa Monica*, twelve miles north of Harlingen, Texas, was my *alma mater*. Harlingen is in far South Texas just thirty miles from the Mexican border. We would ride the bus to school in the mornings and from school in the afternoons even though we lived within walking distance. The monstrous yellow bus with its bustling, noisy cargo thrilled and excited us.

Mother always offered a choice of breakfasts, and as I dressed for school a variety of appetizing smells filled our house. Her *Taquitos*, tender flour *tortilla* roll ups filled with *Papas con Huevo, Huevos con Chorizo, Huevos con Frijoles,* or *Machacado* were best to start the day.

At school, lunch was the exciting time of the day. We children, four brothers, Sam, Eddie, Ralph, and Mike, and I had the option of either bringing a sack lunch to school or walking home to eat. When mama prepared a sack lunch, it was — in season — often of fried rabbit. We were introduced to *Conejo Frito* early in life and relished it. Daddy enjoyed hunting cottontail and jackrabbit which were plentiful in our area. Daddy would take his gun and in his pickup drive to check on his fields and pastures late in the afternoons. As the sun set and it grew darker, rabbits would come from cover of the brush to forage in the grassy open spaces. There they fell easy prey to his gun while frozen stockstill in the blinding

1

lights of the truck. (a process not unlike the "spotlighting" of the illegal poacher and hunter of South Texas with his handheld, battery powered spotlight used on deer and larger game.) Papa would bring his kill of conejos (cottontail) and liebres (jackrabbit) home and we would all help him to skin and gut each rabbit carefully not to taint the meat.

The cottontail were usually fried and the jackrabbits were used for chili meat. Jackrabbit meat is dark, tough, stringy and has a gamier flavor than cottontail. For this reason it is preferred for chili meat. Rabbit is best in spring and early summer and at school I could hardly wait for lunch hour to eat our fried rabbit. Our lunch was communal. I shared with my brothers and the school principal, Simon Gomez. Invariably Principal Gomez on his rounds at lunch would come to our table and ask what we were having. I would always reply, "fried chicken". He knew it was mama's best fried rabbit, and never refused a sample.

Walking home for lunch was no chore. We never knew what mother was going to prepare but whatever it was, one could be sure it was going to be mouth watering. Her luncheon specialties were *Pollo con Arroz, Pollo con Calabaza, Pollo Guisado, Carne con Papas,* or *Fideo con Carne.* She always had flour tortillas to go with her succulent dishes. Freshly cooked beans or *Frijoles Refritos* added the final touch. All it took was a whiff from mama's *cocina,* to pique an instant appetite.

An afterschool snack was dessert for us. We seldom had dessert with a meal because our Mexican tradition was to have a *merienda.* A *merienda* is served in the afternoon and combines rich sweets and a beverage. The type of beverage would depend on the weather, if cold, we were served *Champurado* or hot cocoa, and if hot, cold milk or limeade. As we alighted from the school bus we were greeted by the cinnamony smell of goodies from the oven. It was a pleasant secure feeling to walk into the house knowing mother was in the *cocina.* She would

2

usually have *Fritas, Empanadas, Tamales de Elote, Tortillas de Azucar,* or *Pan de Levadura* ready for us to enjoy.

As I grew older dinnertime came to have special meaning for me because I was allowed to help around the kitchen. Mother would set out her *molcajete* and *tejolote* (a functional and vital utensil in the Mexican *cocina*) equivalent to mortar and pestle. The *molcajete* is carved from volcanic rock and must be properly broken in before being used for the first time. Cracked corn or uncooked rice is used for smoothing the stone. My duty was to grind the garlic, *pimienta* (peppercorns), and *comino* (cumin seed), in the *molcajete.* A small amount of water was added to make it possible to pour from the mortar. These spices are the secret to the rich aromas that flavor Mexican dishes. I would watch mother as she cut up and sautéed chicken or other meat with vegetables and prepared her thickening agent for the dishes. Cooking was an art with her, and she always performed it gracefully, joyously, and continuously for our family. I studied her methods and style and every detail of her cooking procedures. Her dinner specialties included *Carne Guisada, Tacos, Pollo en Salsa, Chuletas de Puerco Rancheras, Repollo con Carne, Enchiladas* or *Chalupas.*

My dad, Samuel Montalvo, owned a meat market and October was usually our time for butchering. Dad and the boys would butcher a young calf late in the fall. It was important to butcher at this time because it was cool and flies would not be numerous. The meat could "ripen" well before refrigerating it. (The "ripening" process allows the meat to cool naturally before refrigeration and then through a period of cooling it improves the flavor and tenderness.) This was perfect weather for preparing *carne seca,* beef jerky. The meat was hung on a line to dry. A large fire would be built so that there would be plenty of coals for *Tripas Asadas,* and *Mollejas.* These were delicacies prepared only at butchering time.

Mother would prepare her gourmet dishes such as *Grillada* (liver and beef stew), *Morcilla* (heart, liver, and beef cubes baked in a calf's *caujo*, an organ located close to its stomach, the rennent bag). It is especially delicious baked in this rennent bag because it has a self basting fatty tissue on the inside, and the ingredients are most tender and flavorful.

Cabeza en Barbacoa, baked beef head, was usually baked in *pozo*, a deep hole in the ground. The head is skinned, rinsed thoroughly and baked in its entirety. (The brains, tongue, and eyes remain in it.) The head is rubbed with butter and wrapped in cheesecloth, then placed in a moist gunny sack. The hole is filled one-third full with hot coals and covered with prickly pear pads (the thorns having been singed off by hot coals). (Prickly pear is used because of its water content. It provides moist heat and prevents coals from scorching the head.) The head is placed over the pear; then the hole is covered with a piece of tin, and dirt shoveled over the tin to seal it. A fire is built over the sealed hole. (The heat over the hole bakes the head.) The head bakes 10-12 hours, and the fire is kept briskly burning. The *Barbacoa* is tender, rich, and delicious.

Menudo, beef tripe stew, is made from the calf's stomach. The stomach is cleaned and boiled to make it easy to scrape the lining. It is washed and cut into cubes, and then used for the smacking dish. (*Menudo* is believed to prevent a hangover if eaten after excessive drinking.) Stacks of corn *tortillas* would be prepared to accompany the savory dishes.

Christmas was a time of festivities for family, relatives, and neighbors. The celebration would start on the 24th with the butchering of a hog. Everybody took part in the joyous event. The hustle and bustle in the kitchen would start in preparation for the *tamalada*, a community get-together specifically to make *tamales* in large quantities for Christmas-eating and sharing. *Tamales de Puerco, Chorizo, Puerco Hornado en Adobe,* and *Chicharrones* would be prepared. *Chicharrones* were interestingly enough prepared by the men. A large cast iron cooking kettle, *olla*, was filled with large cubes of pork fat and pork loin, and as they cooked, they all fried in their own lard. Pork skins would also be stripped and cut 3" x 3" squares and deep fat fried in this rich pork grease. The kettle was placed outdoors in a comfortable area where the men, keeping a close watch over the *olla*, would occasionally stir the *chicharrones*. Potatoes were peeled, cut up in fourths, and fried in the hot fat to keep the lard pure and help retain its creamy white color when stored. (The fried potates were a treat for the children.) The lard was allowed to cool and then stored in cans for future use.

New Year's Eve was celebrated with games, riddles and verses, fireworks, and plenty of *Buñuelos Turcos, Champurado*, and *Té Canela*.

Being Catholic, we observed the Lenten season devoutly. Fridays were special days since we could eat no meat, mother made us forget all about it with her meatless preparations of *Albondigas de Camaron, Atole Pinole, Sopa de Pan, Capirotada*, and *Nopalitos*.

Preparing *nopalitos* during Lent was a family event. The outing would usually occur in the afternoon. Two older sisters, Romie and Rory, my brothers, mother, and I would go out into the South Texas countryside, into the chaparral and mesquite, to collect the prickly pear pads. The prickly pear used for this dish had to be the new growth of the fleshy, heavy pads of the cactus. (Plentiful in March and April.) As we collected them in a bucket, we would layer the prickly pear alternately with mesquite leaves, to prevent thorns from coming into contact with other prickly pear. We would locate a level shady spot with large smooth rocks and flat stumps on which to sit. We would sit in a circle talking while removing thorns from the prickly pear with paring knives and being watchful and apprehensive of rattlesnakes. We would return home with the thorn-free *nopalitos,* and mother would take over their cooking. I sat quietly fascinated as I watched mother transform those green prickly pears into regal food.

Church functions were wonderful. *Cabrito*, young kid, was usually prepared for these events. At our house, mother prepared this meat in many ways: *Cabrito al Carbon* (on spit or over coals), *Machitos*, and *Cabrito Guisado*. *Pan de Campo, Pollo en Mole, Sopa de Arroz, Frijoles a la Mexicana, Guacamole, Pan de Polvo,* and *Chocolate de Boda* were other favorites.

The exposure to my mother's art of Mexican cookery in South Texas has helped me to develop a love of this facet of Mexican culture. It is a heritage that has been passed down from generation to generation. I am now a home economics teacher. The majority of my students are of Mexican descent, and I feel compelled to pass along traditional recipes and values to them in the hope that they may see the true heritage of the South Texas Mexican-American. I pray this book will be one of the means of perpetuating this heritage so that it may never die or be forgotten.

Naranja dulce, limon partido — Dame un abrazo, que yo te pido.

Este Niño Chiquito

Este niño chiquito y bonito
compró un huevito
Este lo quebró,
Este lo batió
Este lo echó al comal
Y éste gordo se lo comió.

6

Antojitos

(Appetizers)

BOTANA
(Pickled Mushrooms)

2-12 oz. cans whole mushrooms (drained)
1 medium can pickled jalapeno, mild

1. Combine drained mushrooms with pickled jalapeno and liquid.
2. Place in a tightly covered plastic container and store in refrigerator.
3. Allow 3-5 days for complete marination and mellowing of mixture.
4. Serve as an appetizer, along with salads, or accompaniment to main dishes.

CHICHARRONES
(Pork Cracklings)

4 lbs. pork loin   Salt to taste
Pure lard   Chili powder

1. Cut pork meat into 2½" cubes.
2. Fry in deep fat fryer with pure lard, until golden brown. Cubes will shrink to half the size.
3. Drain. Sprinkle with salt and chili powder if desired. Favorite cold weather appetizer.
4. Serves 10-12.

CHILE CON QUESO
(Chili Cheese Dip)

1½ lbs. Velveeta cheese
1 1 can tomato and green chili sauce

1. Cut cheese in four chunks.
2. Combine cheese and sauce in double boiler over low heat.
3. Stir often to blend until cheese melts.
4. Keep warm in fondue pot.
5. Serve with chips.

FRIJOLES REFRITOS CON JALAPEÑO
(Jalapeno Bean Dip)

3 cups pinto beans, cooked and mashed
3 tablespoons bacon drippings
1 tablespoon flour
1 teaspoon salt
¼ cup pickled jalapeno peppers, seeded, and minced

1. In skillet heat bacon drippings, add flour and brown.
2. Add mashed beans, minced jalapeno and season with salt. Simmer for 5-10 minutes.
3. Serve with tortilla chips.

GUACAMOLE
(Spicy Avocado Dip)

3 large ripe avocados
1 large tablespoon lemon juice
1½ teaspoon salt
1 tablespoon minced onion
1 large tomato, diced
1 small fresh green chili

1. Cut avocadoes in half and remove pit. Scoop out pulp with a spoon.
2. In a large mortar (molcajete), mash avocados, onion, tomato, and chili. (Mocajete gives it a delicate spicy flavor.)
3. Add lemon juice and salt, mix thoroughly.
4. Serve with corn chips.

9

NACHOS
(Jalapeno Appetizer)

6   corn tortillas
½ cup oil

24 jalapeno slices, thinly
   sliced
2   cups American cheese

1. Cut tortillas into four wedges.
2. Fry tortillas until crisp in oil. Drain.
3. Place tortilla wedges on cookie sheet.
4. Sprinkle grated cheese over each wedge, and top with jalapeno slice.
5. Bake at 200° until cheese melts. Serve hot.
6. Serves 6-8.
7. Corn tortillas can be substituted by ready made tortilla chips, and steps 1 and 2 should be omitted.

PANCHOS
(Jalapeno Plus Appetizer)

6   corn tortillas
½ cup oil
1   cup refried beans

24 jalapeno slices, thinly
   sliced
2   cups grated American
   cheese

1. Cut each tortilla into four wedges.
2. Fry tortillas until crisp in oil. Drain.
3. Place tortilla wedges on cookie sheet.
4. Spread refried beans over each wedge, sprinkle grated cheese, and top with a jalapeno slice.
5. Bake at 200° until cheese melts. Serve hot.
6. Serves 6-8.

PICADILLO
(Mexican Hash Dip)

½ lb. ground beef
½ lb. ground pork
¼ bell pepper, chopped
4 tomatoes, peeled and chopped
1 tablespoon minced onions
2 cloves garlic

1 small can tomato paste
2 jalapenos, chopped
1 pkg. chopped pecans or slivered almonds
1 cup raisins
1 cup water
Salt to taste

1. Brown meat and drain excess fat.
2. Grind onion and garlic in mortar and add water to pour out paste. Add to meat.
3. Add remaining water, and other ingredients.
4. Simmer for 30-40 minutes.
5. Serve hot with corn chips.

QUESADILLAS
(Tortilla Cheese Foldovers)

1 doz. corn tortillas
Butter

12 slices Jack cheese

1. Heat tortillas in shallow butter only long enough to soften. Drain.
2. Place a slice of cheese on the center of each tortilla and fold in half.
3. Place foldovers, side by side on large preheated (200°) griddle.
4. Heat each side for 2 minutes or until cheese melts.
5. Serves 6-8.
6. Popular cook-out appetizer. Quesadillas are also prepared over the grill.

☆   ☆   ☆

Me gusta la leche, me gusta el cafe, pero mas me gustan los ojos de usted.

11

TOSTADAS
(Crisp-Fried Tortillas)

1 doz. corn tortillas   Oil
Salt to taste

1. Fry tortillas, one at a time, in about ½" hot oil.
2. Fry tortillas flat until crisp. Turn once. Use medium heat for frying tortillas to prevent toughening.
3. Drain flat on a paper towel.
4. Sprinkle with salt.
5. Tostadas are served plain or topped with chicken, cheese, chopped tomato, shredded lettuce, sour cream, dressing and avocado.

TURCOS
(Favorite Christmas Foldovers)

Filling:	Dough:
2 lbs. ground pork loin	3 cups flour
1 teaspoon cooking oil	1½ teaspoons salt
1 jar mincemeat	1 cup shortening
1 cup pecans, chopped	12 tablespoons water
1 cup raisins, chopped	

Tea Mixture:

1 cup brown sugar	1 cinnamon stick
8 whole peppercorns, ground	

1. Boil ingredients in 2 cups water.
2. Strain.
3. Add to meat, pecans, and raisins.

Filling:

1. Brown meat in oil, stirring occasionally.
2. Add *mincemeat, pecans and raisins.
3. Simmer mixture 20-25 minutes.
4. Set aside to cool.
5. *Mincemeat may be substituted for tea mixture. (Omit mincemeat if using tea mixture).

(Continued)

12

Dough:

1. Combine flour and salt.
2. Cut in shortening with pastry blender.
3. Make well in center and add water all at once.
4. Stir with fork until mixture becomes dough.
5. Shape dough into dough ball. Pinch off small amounts of dough and shape into small round patties.
6. Roll out on a lightly floured board and spoon cooled meat filling across edge of round. Rolly jelly-roll fashion, starting at edge nearest filling.
7. Roll-overs should be placed seams side up on cookie sheet. Bake at 400° for 15-20 minutes.

Patito, Patito.
Color de café
Me gusta la leche,
Me gusta el café
Pero Más me gustan
los ojos de usted.

13

VERSITOS PARA ÑINOS
(Verses For Children)

A Brincar

Brinca, brinca, brinca alto.
Brinca, brinca de un salto.
1, 2, 3, 4, 5.
Otra vez da un brinco.
6, 7, 8, 9. 10.
Brinca, brinca, otra vez.

El Barquito

En alta mar vi un barquito;
Mareado y muy tristecito.
El capitán furioso reñegaba,
porque el barquito no caminaba.

El Sol

Por aquí sale el sol.
Por acá se mete.
Y cuando llueve
hace soquete.

La Gallina Colorada

La galinna colorada
puso un huevo en el arado,
puso 1, puso 2, puso 3,
puso 4, puso5, puso 6,
puso 7, puso 8, puso 9,
puso 10. La gallina
colorada puso 10, puso 10,
puso 10.

Caballito Mío

Caballito mío,
noble comañero,
porque te conozco,
por eso te quiero.

El Cuento Del Gato

Este era un gato,
con los pies de trapo
y la barriguita al revés.
¿ Quiéres que te lo cuente
otra vez?

Pescadito

Pescadito, pescadito,
¿ No sabes nadar?
Si te saco del agua,
te pondrás a llorar.

Mi Mamita

Mi buena mamita
me lleva a la mesa,
me da la sopita,
y luego me besa.

Mi Tambor

¡ Atención! Atención!
¡ Todos vamos a marchar
al compás de mi tambór!
Tam tam tam, tam tam tam.
¡ Listos todos! Adelante!
A marchar con rigor.
¡ Tam tam tam, tam tam tam!

Mi Avioncito

Yo tengo un avioncito,
color rojo y nuevecito.
Y cuando por las nubes va de
    prisa,
me lleno de sonrisa.

Bebidas

(Beverages)

CHAMPURADO
(Original Mexican Cocoa)

2 quarts milk	1 teaspoon vanilla
½ cup cocoa	¼ cup corn meal
1 cup sugar	½ cup milk
3 -2" cinnamon sticks	

1. In saucepan combine milk and cinnamon sticks. Heat until almost boiling.
2. Combine cocoa, sugar, corn meal and ½ cup milk. Stir to make a thick sauce.
3. Pour cocoa sauce into heated milk stirring constantly with a wire whip or a rotary beater. (5 minutes)
4. Serve at once. Very delicious served with sopapillas or bunuelos. Serves 8-10.

CHOCOLATE DE BODA
(Mexican Wedding Hot Chocolate)

4 cups milk	3 -2" cinnamon sticks
5 oz. semisweet chocolate	1 teaspoon vanilla

1. In saucepan, combine milk, semisweet chocolate, and cinnamon.
2. Cook and stir just until chocolate melts.
3. Remove from heat; stir in vanilla.
4. Beat vigorously and serve in mugs. Serves 4.

LIMONADA
(Limeade)

2 quarts water	Marachino cherries
1 cup sugar	Lime slices
Juice of 6 limes	Ice cubes

1. Combine water and sugar. Stir until sugar dissolves.
2. Add lime juice and ice cubes.
3. Pour into glasses and garnish with slice of lime and cherry.

MARGARITA
(Favorite Mexican Tequila Drink)

2 oz. Tequila
1 oz. Triple Sec

3 oz. lemon juice (or lime juice)

1. Prepare salt rim on glass by dipping edge of glass ½" deep into lime juice, then into coarse salt.
2. Mix ingredients, shake with shaved ice and serve in salt-rimmed glass.
3. Serves 2-3.

SANGRIA
(Mexican Spiked Punch)

2 quarts red wine
1 cup orange juice
4 tablespoons lime juice
⅔ cup sugar
½ cup Cointreau or Curacoa

2 bottles 12 oz. Club soda, chilled
Ice cubes
Orange slices
Lime slices

1. In a large pitcher combine wine, orange and lime juices with the sugar. Stir until sugar is dissolved.
2. Add liqueur. Chill.
3. Just before serving add club soda, ice cubes, and garnish with orange and lime slices.
4. Serves 10-12.

TÉ DE ANISE
(Anise Seed Tea)

4 cups water
2 teaspoons anise seed

3 tablespoons sugar

1. Bring water to a boil. Add anise seeds and steep for 10-15 minutes. Strain tea.
2. Add sugar and stir until dissolved.
3. Serve as a beverage. Sometimes it is used as a liquid in some recipes.

TÉ DE CANELA
(Cinnamon Tea)

3	-2" cinnamon sticks	3	tablespoons sugar
4	cups water		

1. Bring cinnamon and water to a boil. Reduce heat and simmer 15-20 minutes.
2. Add sugar and stir until dissolved. Tea should have a dark reddish color and a spicy aroma.
3. Strain and serve in mugs.
4. This tea is a popular delicious Mexican beverage. It is also known to have medicinal values. It will relieve menstrual cramps.

TÉ DE LLERBA BUENA
(Mint Tea)

4	cups water	3	tablespoons sugar
1	tablespoon mint, fresh or dried		

1. Bring water to a boil. Add mint leaves and steep for 5-10 minutes. Strain tea.
2. Add sugar and stir until dissolved.
3. Serve as a beverage. It also has medicinal value. It is known to relieve indigestion or heartburn.

Corriendo, corriendo, me di un trompezon — por darte la mano te di el carazon.

RIDDLE (ADIVINANZA)

Es su madre tartamuda
y su padre buen cantor;
tiene el vestidito blanco
y amarillo el corazón.

(El huevo)

Caldos, Ensaladas, Salsas, Y Legumbres

(Soups, Salads, Sauces, and Vegetables)

Picante

Nachos

CALDO DE POLLO
(Chicken Soup)

1	4½-5 lb. stewing chicken, cut up	1	cup carrots, sliced circles
1	tablespoon salt	¼	cup celery, diced
2	quarts water	2	cups potatoes, cubed
1	teaspoon mixed spices (peppercorn and cumin)	1	garlic clove
			tomato, chopped (optional)

1. In 4-quart Dutch oven combine chicken, water, salt, and spices. Bring to boiling. Reduce heat; simmer, covered, for 20 minutes.
2. Add remaining ingredients. Simmer 20 minutes.
3. Serve with *Tortilla De Masa* or *Tortillas De Manteca.*
4. Serves 6-8.

CALDO DE RES
(Beef Bone and Vegetable Soup)

2	lbs. soup bone	2	garlic cloves
2	tablespoons cooking oil	2	teaspoons mixed spices (peppercorns and cumin)
1	teaspoon salt	¼	cup elbow macaroni or rice
2	pkgs. soup mix (fresh vegetables)		Water
	tomato, optional		

1. In soup pot heat oil and brown beef cubes and bone. Add salt. Cover and simmer 10 minutes.
2. Wash, peel, and chop vegetables and add to beef. Flavors will begin to blend and give off an appetizing aroma.
3. Grind spices and garlic. Add a little water and add to soup mixture. Add enough water to cover all ingredients. Simmer for 40 minutes.
4. Add elbow macaroni, rice or noodles if desired. Soup is ready to serve as soon as macaroni is tender.
5. Serve with hot corn tortillas. Serves 6-8.

☆   ☆   ☆

Pon, pon, la manita en el bordon saca medio para el jabon
    Para lavar el pantalon.

FRIJOLES A LA MEXICANA
(Original Mexican Bean Soup)

3 cups dry pinto beans	2 fresh green chili peppers
1 cup salt pork, cubed (or bacon rind)	2 cans whole tomatoes
3 garlic cloves	2 quarts water
½ onion, chopped	Salt to taste
2 cups fresh Coriander, minced (*cilantro*)	

1. Pick and wash pinto beans. Drain.
2. In large cooking pot heat 2 quarts water. Add dry beans, salt pork, and garlic. Cover and simmer 2 hours.
3. Add onion, coriander, chili peppers, and whole tomatoes. Cover and simmer 2 hours or until beans are tender. Add salt to taste.
4. Serve as an appetizer, side dish or snack. Serves 10-12.

FRIJOLES REFRITOS
(Refried Beans)

3 cups pinto beans, cooked and mashed	1 teaspoon salt
3 tablespoons bacon drippings	¼ teaspoon pepper
	1 tablespoon flour

1. In skillet heat bacon drippings, add flour and brown.
2. Add mashed beans, season with salt and pepper and simmer for 5-10 minutes. If beans seem dry, add bean soup to make refried beans creamy.
3. Serve as a side dish along with rice, or use as a filling for *taquitos*. Serves 4-6.

RIDDLE (ADIVINANZA)

Si soy joven, joven quedo;
si soy viejo, quedo viejo;
tengo boca y no hablo
tengo ojos y no veo.

(El retrato)

21

BURRITOS
(Fried Tortilla-Bean Foldovers)

12   flour tortillas, rolled 7"
      diameter, uncooked
6   slices American cheese

3   cups refried beans
    Oil for frying

1. Spoon 2 tablespoons refried beans in center of each tortilla. Top with ½ of a slice of cheese.
2. Fold one side of tortilla over filling and then fold other side over it. Fold ends over in the same way, making about a 4" square *burrito*. Store in freezer, if desired.
3. Drop immediately into deep fat. Fry for about 5-8 minutes, turning *burritos* to brown them on all sides.
4. Drain on absorbent paper and serve at once.
5. Serve with *chili con carne* over *burritos*.
6. Makes 12 *burritos*.

CHALUPAS
(Bean Tostadas)

8-10 corn tortillas
Oil
3   cups refried beans
   ½ lettuce head, shredded

2   cups grated American
    Cheese
3   chopped tomatoes

1. Fry tortillas flat until crisp. Drain.
2. Place on cookie sheet and spread beans over each tostada, and top with grated cheese.
3. Bake at 300° until cheese melts. Serve hot.
4. Top with shredded lettuce and chopped tomatoes.
5. Serves 5-8.

RIDDLE (ADIVINANZA)

Fui a la plaza
compré de ella
vine a mi casa
y lloré con ella.

(La cebolla)

CHILES RELLENOS
(Stuffed Green Peppers)

6 whole green chiles	3 eggs, separated
1 pkg. 8 oz. Jack Cheese	3 tablespoons flour
½ cup flour, seasoned with	Oil for frying
Salt and pepper	

1. Slit chiles lengthwise, just enough to remove seeds. Boil for 10 minutes just enough to tenderize chiles. Drain.
2. Cut cheese into strips ½" thick and long enough to fit into chiles. Stuff each chile with a strip of cheese.
3. Dredge stuffed chiles in seasoned flour. Set aside.
4. Beat egg whites until stiff peaks form.
5. Beat eggs yolks until creamy. Fold yolks into whites adding 3 tablespoons flour as you fold.
6. Dip each stuffed chile into this batter and set on a small dish.
7. Slide coated chile from dish into deep hot oil to fry (400°). Fry until golden brown, turning once gently. (2 minutes)
8. Drain *rellenos* on paper towels.
9. Serve with Mexican rice, refried beans, avocado salad, and corn tortillas.

SOPA DE ARROZ
(Tasty Mexican Rice)

1 cup rice, uncooked	¼ cup onion, chopped
⅓ cup cooking oil	¼ cup green bell pepper
1 medium can tomato sauce	chopped
or 2 tomatoes chopped	2 teaspoons salt
2 cloves garlic	4 cups boiling water or
1½ teaspoon mixed spices	broth
(peppercorn and cumin)	

1. Grind spices and garlic. Add a little water and set aside.
2. In skillet heat oil and brown rice.
3. Add spices, tomato sauce, bell pepper, onion, salt, and boiling water. Simmer 20 minutes (stir only once during the simmering process).
4. Serves 6-8.

SOPA DE FIDEO
(Vermicelli Side Dish)

1 -10 oz. pkg. Vermicelli
⅓ cup cooking oil
1 can whole tomatoes
2 cloves garlic
3 cups boiling water

1 teaspoons mixed spices
   (cumin and peppercorns)
¼ cup bell pepper chopped
2 teaspoons salt

1. Grind garlic and spices. Add a little water and set aside.
2. In skillet on low heat, add oil and break up vermicelli and fry until golden brown.
3. Add spices, tomatoes, bell pepper, salt and boiling water. Simmer 15-20 minutes.
4. Serves 6-8.

ENSALADA MEXICANA
(Mexican Chef Salad)

1 lb. ground beef
1 can kidney beans, drained
1 teaspoon salt
1 head lettuce
4 tomatoes, cut in wedges

½ cup green onions, minced
1 cup grated cheddar cheese
1 cup Italian Salad dressing
1 pkg. corn chips
1 large avocado, peeled and sliced lengthwise

1. Brown ground beef in skillet, add beans and salt. Simmer for 10 minutes. Drain.
2. Combine lettuce, tomatoes, cheese, salad dressing, and corn chips.
3. Add beef and beans, mixing lightly.
4. Garnish with alternate slices of tomato and avocado, making a sunburst effect.
5. Serve with hot sauce, if desired. Serves 6-8.

RIDDLE (ADIVINANZA)

Siempre quietas,
siempre inquietas,
durmiendo de día
y de noche despiertas.

(Las estrellas)

GUACAMOLE
(Spicy Avocado-Tomato Salad)

3 medium avocados, seeded
and peeled
1 fresh large tomato, diced
1 fresh green chili pepper,
minced

¼ cup onion, minced
(optional)
2 teaspoons salt

1. Peel and seed avocados.
2. Grind onion and chili pepper in mortar (*molcajete*). Add avocados and mash. (The mortar gives this salad a delicate spicy taste.)
3. Add diced tomatoes, salt, and mix thoroughly. Serve on mortar or transer to a serving dish.
4. Serve with crisp fried *tostadas*, chips, or hot corn tortillas.

SALSA DE PEPINO SILVESTRE
(Wild Gherkins Chili Sauce)

10 wild gherkins, boiled,
and drained
1 8 oz. can tomato sauce

4-6 fresh green chilipetins
1 clove garlic
1 teaspoon mixed spices
(cumin and peppercorns)

1. Boil wild gherkins in 2 cups water for 20 minutes. Drain.
2. Place all ingredients in a blender. Cover; blend till pureed.
3. Transfer to saucepan; heat through. Makes 6-8 servings.
4. (This sauce may be used to spice up almost any food.)

SALSA PICANTE
(Hot Chili Sauce)

2 large tomatoes, diced
1 clove garlic, small
¼ cup onion, minced
¼ cup fresh coriander,
minced (*cilantro*)

1 teaspoon salt
2 large green chili peppers,
seeded and chopped

1. In mortar grind garlic, onions, and chili peppers.
2. Add tomatoes, coriander, and salt. Mix thoroughly.
3. Use mortar (*molcajete*) as serving dish.
4. (This sauce is excellent served with any Mexican dish or food.) Serves 6-8.

SALSA RANCHERA
(Ranch-Style Sauce)

3	large tomatoes, chopped	2	green chili peppers,
1	tablespoon cooking oil		seeded and minced
½	onion, chopped	1	clove garlic
1	teaspoon salt	1	teaspoon mixed spices (cumin and peppercorns)

1. In skillet saute onion in oil. Add chopped tomatoes, chili peppers, and salt. Simmer 5 minutes.
2. Grind garlic and spices. Add a little water and add to tomato mixture. Simmer 5 minutes.
3. Makes 3-4 servings.

SALSA VERDE
(Green Enchilada Sauce)

6	fresh green *tomatillos*, cooked and chopped	¼	cup fresh coriander (cilantro)
2	green chili peppers, minced	1	teaspoon salt
¼	cup onion, chopped	¼	cup chicken broth

1. (*Tomatillos* are green tomatoes which have a dry husk-like covering.) Remove husk covering, rinse, and boil tomatoes in 2 cups water until tender. Drain and chop tomatoes.
2. Blend tomatoes, onion, chili peppers, coriander, broth, and salt in a blender. Cover; blend till pureed.
3. Transfer to saucepan; heat thoroughly. Serves 3-4.
4. (Use this sauce for Green Enchiladas or Green *Mole* dishes.)

RIDDLE (ADIVINANZA)

Un viejito
No muy viejo
Tiene barbas — no
muy largas
Tiene dientes y
no muerde
¿ Qué es?

(El Ajo)

Carne De Res

(Beef)

ARROZ CON CARNE
(Rice and Beef Skillet Dinner)

2 cups rice, uncooked	3 teaspoons mixed spices
2 lbs. round roast, cubed	(cumin and peppercorns)
2 tablespoons cooking oil	2 garlic cloves
1 large can whole tomatoes	Boiling water

1. Brown rice in oil.
2. Brown meat, add rice to meat.
3. Grind spices and garlic in mortar (*molcajete*) and add a small amount of water to pour out of mortar. Add to rice.
4. Add canned tomatoes and enough boiling water to cover. Simmer for 30-40 minutes. Stir only once during the simmering process.
5. Serves 8-10.

CARNE CON PAPAS
(Potato-Beef Hash)

3-4 medium potatoes, cubed	1 tablespoon salt
1½ lbs. chuck steak, cubed	2 cloves garlic
3 tablespoons cooking oil	1 teaspoon mixed spices
1 can whole tomatoes	(peppercorns and cumin)
3 cups water	

1. Brown potatoes and add salt.
2. Add beef cubes to browned potatoes. Stir, cover, simmer for 20 minutes.
3. Grind spices and garlic and add a little water to mortar.
4. Add spices, tomatoes, and water to meat and potatoes.
5. Simmer 20 minutes.

RIDDLE (ADIVINANZA)

Un buque chiquito
Forado de plata
Que vive y navega
En agua salada
¿ Que es?

(Un pez)

28

CARNE GUISADA
(Mexican Cowboy Stew)

4	lbs. round roast, cubed	1	medium can tomato sauce
1	tablespoon cooking oil	2	teaspoons salt
2	teaspoons mixed spices (cumin and peppercorns)	2	tablespoons flour-½ cup water
2	garlic cloves		

1. Cut meat in cubes and brown in oil. Add salt.
2. Grind spices and garlic in mortar (*molcajete*) and add a small amount of water to pour out of the mortar.
3. Add spices, tomato sauce, and enough water to cover sauteed meat.
4. Simmer for 30-40 minutes.
5. Blend flour and water. Stir into meat to make gravy.
6. Simmer 10 minutes.
7. Serves 8-10. (Serve with flour tortillas.)

CARNE PICADA CON ELOTE
(Hamburger-Corn Supreme)

2	lbs. hamburger meat	½	cup tomato sauce
1	tablespoon cooking oil	2	teaspoons salt
1	clove garlic	1	can whole kernel corn
1	teaspoon mixed spices (cumin and peppercorns)	2	tablespoons flour-½ cup water

1. Grind garlic and mixed spices, add a little water and set aside.
2. Brown meat in oil. Add salt.
3. Add spices and tomato sauce. Cover; simmer 20 minutes.
4. Add corn, and flour paste. (2 tablespoons flour and ½ cup water is blended together to make flour paste to thicken mixture.)
5. (Green beans can be substituted for corn.) Stir and simmer for 10-15 minutes.
6. Serves 6-8.

CARNE SECA
(Beef Jerky)

3 lbs. lean beef, any cut	Salt
1 cup steak sauce or lemon juice	Pepper

1. Cut meat with grain (lengthwise) about 1 inch wide and ¼ inch thick.
2. Place in a shallow pan. Cover with sauce. Marinate for two hours.
3. Remove meat strips, sprinkle with salt and pepper, and place crosswise on oven racks. (Line bottom of oven with foil.)
4. Dry in oven 9-12 hours at 140°.

CHILE CON CARNE
(Zesty Mexican Chili)

4 lbs. hamburger meat	4 tablespoons flour
1 tablespoon salt	1 cup water
4 cups water	3 cups pinto beans, cooked and drained (optional)
4 tablespoons chili powder	

1. In large soup pot, combine beef and water by using hand to break up meat in the water completely. Add salt.
2. Simmer over low heat for 20 minutes, and stir occasionally.
3. Mix chili powder, flour, and water and make a paste. Add to meat and stir.
4. Simmer, covered, stirring occasionally until chili is thick, about 30-40 minutes.
5. Add cooked pinto beans if desired.
6. Serves 10-15.

RIDDLE (ADIVINANZA)

Chiquito como un arador
sube a la mesa del emperador

(La sal)

CONCHITAS CON CARNE
(Shell Macaroni-Beef Dish)

1½ lbs. hamburger meat
2 tablespoons cooking oil
1 pkg. shell macaroni
1 can whole tomatoes
1½ cups hot water

1 teaspoon mixed spices
   (cumin and peppercorns)
2 cloves garlic
2 teaspoons salt

1. Brown shell macaroni in oil; add meat and stir until meat browns. Add salt.
2. Grind garlic and mixed spices in mortar (*molcajete*), add water, and pour into meat mixture.
3. Add tomatoes and hot water. Cover and simmer for 30-40 minutes.
4. Serves 4-6.

COSTILLAS GUISADAS
(Savory Braised Spareribs)

3 lbs. spareribs, cut in riblets
2 tablespoons cooking oil
2 teaspoons salt
2 cloves garlic
½ cup water

1½ teaspoons mixed spices
   (peppercorns and cumin)
1½ cups warm water
2 tablespoons flour

1. Grind garlic and spices, add a little water and set aside.
2. Brown spareribs in oil. Add salt, spices, and warm water. Cover and simmer for 40 minutes.
3. Mix flour and water to make a paste. (2 tablespoons flour and ½ cup water) Add to spareribs and stir. (This should make a thick gravy.)
4. Simmer 15-20 minutes. Serves 4-6.

RIDDLE (ADIVINANZA)

Blanco de casa salí
en el campo enverdecí
y blanco a casa volví
¿ Qué es?

(El maíz)

ENCHILADAS
(Rolled Saucy-Filled Corn Tortillas)

Enchilada Sauce:

3	tablespoons cooking oil	3	tablespoons flour
2	tablespoons chili powder	2	cups water

1. Lightly brown flour in oil, add chili powder and stir constantly for one minute. Remove from heat.
2. Add water gradually and stir until well blended and a creamy sauce.
3. Place back on low heat and cook until thick.

Meat Filling: (Use *Chili Con Carne* recipe for filling.)

12 corn tortillas		Enchilada filling (*Chili*)
Oil for frying	3	cups grated American
Enchilada Sauce		cheese

1. Lift tortillas, one at a time, with kitchen tongs and dip in ½" heated oil in skillet. (Heat tortilla just for a few seconds, only long enough to soften.)
2. Lift tortilla from oil and dip immediately into heated enchilada sauce.
3. Add filling on the center of the tortilla, sprinkle cheese, and then roll. (Rolled enchiladas should be placed seam side down in serving dish to keep filling in place.)
4. Spoon 2 tablespoons of Enchilada Sauce evenly over each tortilla and sprinkle on remaining cheese. Bake 350° for 20 minutes.

RIDDLE (ADIVINANZA)

Soy redondo
Soy amarillo
Doy luz
Doy calor
Y a las cosas
Doy color
Adivina lo que soy

(El sol)

TACOS
(Crisp-Filled Corn Tortillas)

Taco Shells:

12 corn tortillas   Oil for frying

1. In a heavy skillet, in about ½" hot oil fry tortillas, one at a time.
2. As the tortilla softens, gently lift edge with tongs and start to unfold upward and over to form a half circle shape. (Do not make a sharp fold.) Fry until crisp.
3. Keep shells warm in oven at 150°.

Filling:

1 tablespoon oil	1 clove garlic
1½ lbs. hamburger meat	1 teaspoon mixed spices
¼ cup onion	(cumin and peppercorns)
2 tomatoes, chopped	1½ teaspoons salt
2 cups finely shredded	
lettuce and diced tomatoes	

1. In oil, saute meat, onion, and tomatoes. Add salt.
2. Grind spices and garlic in mortar. Add to meat mixture.
3. Simmer for 15 minutes. Make flour paste to thicken meat mixture. (2 tablespoons flour and ½ cup water.) Add to mixture and stir.
4. Simmer 8-10 minutes. Fill taco shells with cooked meat, topped with shredded lettuce and diced tomatoes. (For chicken tacos substitute 4 cups diced cooked chicken for beef.) Serves 4-6.

☆　☆　☆

Las Hojitas
(verso para el otoño)

Las hojitas, las hojitas
De los árboles se caen
Viene el viento
y las levanta
y se ponen a jugar.

FIDEO CON CARNE
(Vermicelli-Beef Delight)

1½ lbs. chuck steak, cubed
3 tablespoons cooking oil
¼ cup bell pepper, chopped
2 cloves garlic

1 teaspoon mixed spices (peppercorns and cumin)
1 10 oz. pkg. vermicelli
1 can whole tomatoes

1. Grind garlic and mixed spices, add a little water and set aside.
2. Break up vermicelli, and in low heat fry in oil until golden brown. Add salt.
3. Brown meat cubes, add vermicelli to meat.
4. Add spices, tomatoes, and chopped bell peppers. Add boiling water and cover. (Add enough water to cover) Simmer 30-40 minutes.
5. (Rice could be substituted for vermicelli.) Use 1 cup uncooked rice if preferred. Chicken could be substituted for beef.
6. Serves 6-8.

Comidas De Gastronomo

(Gourmet Foods)

BARBACOA DE CABEZA
(Beef Head Bar-B-Que)

Beef Head   Salt
Butter   Pepper

1. Rub entire head with butter, salt, and pepper. Wrap with foil.
2. Bake at low even 250° for 8-10 hours.
3. Remove all meat from head bones.
4. Serve meat, tongue, and brains with chili sauce and hot flour or corn tortillas.
5. (Head can be prepared in a *pozo* as described in the introduction.)

CABRITO AL CARBON
(Roasted Kid Goat)

1   15 lb. kid goat, quartered   ½ cup cooking oil
1   tablespoon salt   ½ cup water

1. Combine salt, oil, and water for basting.
2. Roast over medium coals 1½-2 hours. Turn every 15 minutes till done. Baste frequently.
3. (If rotisserie is available. Adjust *cabrito* on rotisserie. Rotate over slow coals 2 hours or until done. Baste frequently.)
4. (To roast in oven wrap meat in foil and place in shallow pan. Roast at 300° for 1 hour. Brown, uncovered 15-20 minutes at 350°.
5. Season with salt. Serves 8-10.

CABRITO GUISADO
(Favorite Fiesta Stew)

4	lbs. kid goat meat, cubed	1	small can tomato sauce
1	tablespoon cooking oil	2	teaspoons salt
4	teaspoons mixed spices	2	tablespoons flour-
	(peppercorns and cumin)		½ cup water
3	garlic cloves		

1. Cut meat in cubes and brown in oil. Add salt.
2. Grind spices and garlic and add a small amount of water.
3. Add spices, tomato sauce, and enough water to cover meat.
4. Simmer for 30-40 minutes.
5. Blend flour and water. Stir into meat to make gravy.
6. Simmer 10 minutes. Serves 8-10.
7. (Serve with flour or corn tortillas.)
*8. A traditional blood pudding, *Sangrita*, is also prepared by following this recipe. For Step 5 substitute: 1 cup kid goat blood, mixed with the flour. (Omit the tomato sauce and ½ cup water.)

CONEJO FRITO
(Fried Rabbit)

2	cottontail rabbits, cut into frying pieces	2	teaspoons salt
	½ cup milk	¼	teaspoon black pepper
1	cup flour		Oil for frying

1. Cut rabbit as you would chicken (at the joint of each piece).
2. Dip rabbit pieces in milk, then shake in bag containing flour, salt, and pepper.
3. Allow to stand for about 10 minutes to let coating set.
4. Fry in deep fat or oil until brown and tender. 20-25 minutes.
5. Drain on paper towels before serving. Serves 6-8.

GRILLADA
(Spicy Beef-Liver-Heart Stew)

1½ lbs. round roast, cubed	2 garlic cloves
1 lb. liver, cubed	½ cup tomato sauce
1 lb. heart, cubed	2 teaspoons salt
1 tablespoon oil	2 tablespoons flour-
4 teaspoons minced spices	½ cup water
(cumin and peppercorns)	

1. Cut meat, liver and heart in cubes. Brown in oil. Add salt. Cover and simmer 15-20 minutes.
2. Grind spices, and garlic and add small amount of water.
3. Add spices, tomato sauce, and enough water to cover meat mixture.
4. Simmer 30-40 minutes.
5. Blend flour and water. Stir into meat mixture to make gravy.
6. Simmer 10 minutes until thick and bubbly.
7. Serves 8-10.

LENGUA ENTOMATADA
(Ranch-Style Tongue)

1 beef tongue	¼ cup onion, chopped
1 quart water	1 clove garic
1 large can whole tomatoes	1 teaspoon mixed spices
1 tablespoon cooking oil	(cumin and peppercorns)
2 teaspoons salt	

1. Boil tongue in water until tender 20-30 minutes. Drain.
2. Remove skin layer from tongue and slice tongue ½" thick. Set aside.
3. Grind spices and garlic. Add a small amount of water and set aside.
4. In heated oil saute onions, add whole tomatoes, and spices. Season with salt and simmer 5-10 minutes.
5. Add tongue slices to tomato sauce and simmer 10 minutes. Serve hot.
6. Serves 6-8.

MENUDO
(Beef Tripe Stew)

3 lbs. beef tripe (*menudo*)
2 quarts water
3 cans hominy, drained
2 tablespoons chili powder
Salt to taste

4 teaspoons mixed spices
  (cumin and peppercorns)
3 cloves garlic
2 tablespoons oil

1. Cut tripe in small cubes, rinse, and cook in 2 quarts water until tender. (Do not add salt to water—it toughens tripe.) Drain.
2. Grind spices and garlic in mortar. Add a small amount of water.
3. Brown chili powder in oil, add ground spices (use a large pot).
4. Add cooked tripe, hominy, enough water to cover, and salt to taste.
5. Simmer for 30 minutes. (Serve hot with crackers.) (It may be seasoned with lemon slices, oregano, or chopped onion.)
6. Serves 10-12. (Serve as an appetizer, social dish after a dance, and an early morning dish after a night of partying.) (Better known as "the breakfast of the champions.")

MOLLEJAS ASADAS
(Grilled Sweetbreads)

4 lbs. Sweetbreads (*mollejas*) Salt
Water

1. Boil sweetbreads in water for 15 minutes. Drain. (This prevents shrinkage.)
2. Cook sweetbreads over grill until brown. Cut into serving pieces.
3. Season with salt. Serves 6-8.
4. (Serve as an appetizer with flour or corn tortillas.)

RIDDLE (ADIVINANZA)

Una vieja larga y seca
que le escurre la manteca.

(La vela)

39

MACHITOS

(Gourmet Wrap-Ups)

1 lb. cubed beef or kid goat
(*cabrito*) meat
½ kid goat liver, cubed
½ kid goat heart,
cubed
2 sheets of thin membrane,
Pellicle, or *tela*, (thin interi-
or membrane of the an-
mal's body)

6 feet beef or kid tripe
1 clove garlic
1 teaspoon mixed spices
(peppercorns and cumin)
2 teaspoons salt

1. Grind spices and garlic.
2. In large mixing bowl combine cubed meat, heart, liver, spices, and salt. Mix lightly.
3. Spread membrane sheet (4" x 6") and spoon half of meat mixture, lengthwise near the edge of the membrane.
4. Roll membrane (tela) jelly-roll fashion, starting at edge nearest filling. (Fold in ends before starting to roll so that filling will be sealed inside the membrane.)
5. Take 3 feet of tripe for each roll and wrap it across the roll.
6. Cover the roll completely with the tripe. (Tripe may be omitted if desired. Wrap in foil instead.)
7. Roast over medium coals 1½ hours or grill, turning every 15 minutes.
8. (In oven bake at 300° for 1 hour. Brown, uncovered at 350° for 15-20 minutes.)
9. (These wrap-ups are tasty appetizers. Serve sliced with corn tortillas and chili sauce.) Serves 8-10.

RIDDLE (ADIVINANZA)

En alto vive,
en alto mora,
en alto teje,
la tejedora.

(La araña)

MORCILLA
(Mexican Gourmet Dish)

1   *cuajo* (beef rennet bag or the fourth stomach attached to the stomach)
3   lbs. beef, cubed
3   cups blood (blood may be substituted with ¼ cup flour and 1 cup water mixed into a paste.

1   clove garlic
½   beef heart, cubed
1   large sweetbread, cubed
Salt to taste

1. Grind spices in mortar (molcajete). Add a small amount of water to pour out paste.
2. Mix all ingredients together.
3. Fill *cuajo.* (fatty tissue of organ should be on the inside)
4. Tie with clamps. Place in large Dutch oven. Fill ¼ of container with water.
5. Cover and cook 1-1½ hours.
6. Slice and serve with hot flour tortillas.
7. (Excellent appetizer served with beer.)

POZOLE
(Pigs Feet and Jowl Soup)

6   pigs feet or 2 large jowls
2   cans hominy, drained
2   tablespoon chili powder
1   tablespoon oil

2   teaspoon mixed spices (cumin and peppercorns)
2   cloves garlic
Salt to taste

1. Cook pigs feet in 2 quarts unsalted water. Drain.
2. Grind spices, and garlic in mortar; mix with small amount of water to make paste.
3. Brown chili powder in oil on low heat, add ground spices.
4. Add cooked pigs feet, enough water to cover, and salt to taste. Add hominy.
5. Simmer 30 minutes to allow flavors to blend.
6. Serves 10-12. (Tasty cold weather dish. Serve with crackers.)
7. (Freezes well for 1-2 months.)

NOPALITOS
(Prickly Pear Souffle)

2	cups *nopalitos* (tender baby prickly pears), diced	2	teaspoons salt
2	tablespoons cooking oil	4	eggs
2	tablespoons flour	1	tablespoon chili powder
		½	cup water

1. Remove prickly pear thorns, rinse thoroughly. Dice.
2. Cook diced prickly pear in four cups water for 15 minutes. Rinse. Drain.
3. Grind garlic and spices and add a little water. Set aside.
4. Brown chili powder in oil 1-2 minutes; stir constantly. (Do not scorch!)
5. Add spices and diced prickly pear. Simmer 5-10 minutes. Add salt. Mix flour and water to make a paste. Add to prickly pear.
6. Beat egg whites until soft peaks form. Fold in beaten yolks.
7. Fold egg mixture into *nopalitos* and cook until egg mixture is cooked. (This dish is as light as a souffle.)
8. Serves 6-8. (Serve with corn tortillas.)
9. (If canned prickly pear is used, omit steps 1 and 2. Drain and follow the recipe.)

TRIPAS ASADAS
(Grilled Beef Tripes)

4   lbs. beef tripes (*tripas*)   Salt
Water

1. Cut tripes 6-8" long, rinse, and boil in water for 30 minutes. Drain.
2. Roast over medium coals until brown and crisp.
3. Season with salt. (Serve as appetizers with corn tortillas.)
4. Serves 8-10.

RIDDLE (ADIVINANZA)

Lana sube
lana baja.

(La navaja)

Huevos Y Aves

(Eggs and Poultry)

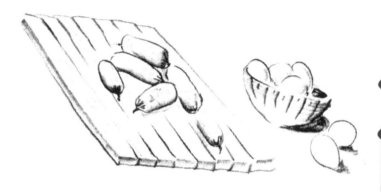

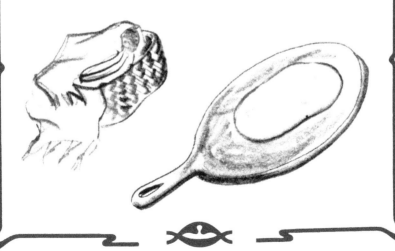

ALBONDIGAS DE CAMARON
(Egg and Shrimp Fritters)

4 eggs	2 tablespoons flour
1½ cups shrimp, cooked and chopped	¼ teaspoon black pepper
	2 teaspoons salt
¼ cup onion, minced	cooking oil

1. In large mixing bowl beat eggs; add onion, salt, black pepper, and shrimp. Mix well.
2. Add flour to egg mixture and blend. This makes a batter.
3. In deep skillet heat 1 inch cooking oil. Pour ¼ cup batter for each fritter into hot oil. Fry, a few at a time, till golden brown, about 1 minute on each side.
4. Drain on paper towels. (Serve hot with *ranchero* sauce, if desired.)
5. Serves 4-6. Makes 8-10 fritters.

CHORIZO CON HUEVO
(Sausage-Egg Scramble)

2 Mexican pork link sausages, remove casing	4 eggs
	2 teaspoons salt
1 teaspoon cooking oil	

1. In skillet cook sausage 5 minutes or till browned, stirring occasionally. (Add 1 teaspoon oil if sausage seems dry.)
2. Add eggs and salt to sausage and stir eggs to combine with sausage.
3. Allow mixture to set on bottom and sides of pan. Stir lightly and cook 5 minutes more or till eggs are cooked but glossy and moist.
4. (Serve with hot flour tortillas or prepare as *taquitos*.)
5. Serves 4-6.

RIDDLE (ADIVINANZA)

Agua pasa por mi casa
cate de mi corazón
el que no me lo adivine
es un burro cabezón.

(Aguacate)

44

ALBONDIGAS DE CARNE SECA
(Egg and Beef Jerky Fritters)

½ lb. beef jerky, chipped
4 eggs
¼ cup onion, minced
¼ cup green pepper, diced

2 tablespoons flour
2 teaspoons salt
¼ teaspoon pepper
Cooking oil

1. Boil jerky 20-30 minutes. Drain and cut up into small chips.
2. In large mixing bowl beat eggs, add onion, green pepper, salt, black pepper, and chipped jerky.
3. Add flour to egg mixture and blend. This makes a batter.
4. In deep skillet heat 1 inch cooking oil. Pour ¼ cup batter for each fritter into hot oil. Fry, a few at a time, till golden brown, about 2 minutes on each side.
5. Drain on paper towels. Serve hot.
6. Serves 4-6. Makes 10-12 fritters.
7. May be served in *meat broth if preferred — (Albondigas En Caldo).

*Meat Broth

Broth (from beef jerky)
1 clove garlic

1 teaspoon mixed spices
(peppercorn and cumin)

1. Use jerky broth and add ground spices and garlic. Simmer 10 minutes.
2. Pour broth over jerky fritters. Serve hot.

HUEVOS CON CHICHARRONES
(Scrambled Eggs with Pork Cracklings)

½ cup pork cracklings, small chunks
3 eggs

1 tablespoon salt
¼ teaspoon black pepper
1 teaspoon cooking oil

1. In skillet heat oil and saute pork cracklings.
2. Add eggs, salt and black pepper to cracklings and stir to combine mixture.
3. Allow mixture to set on bottom and sides of pan. Then stir lightly and cook 5 minutes or till eggs are cooked but glossy and moist.
4. Serves 2-4.

HUEVOS CON FRIJOLES
(Eggs and Bean Scramble)

2 tablespoons bacon   ¼ teaspoon black pepper
  drippings   4   eggs
1 cup cooked pinto beans   ¼ cup milk
2 teaspoons salt

1. In skillet heat drippings and add beans. Stir and simmer 3-5 minutes.
2. Beat eggs, milk, salt, and pepper with fork.
3. Pour egg mixture over beans.
4. Stir mixture till it starts to set. ' Stir lightly and cook 5 minutes or till eggs are cooked.
5. Serves 4-6.

HUEVOS FRITOS EN CHILE COLORADO
(Fried Eggs in Zesty Chili Sauce)

1 tablespoon chili powder   2   teaspoons salt
2 tablespoons cooking oil   1   tablespoon water
4 eggs

1. In skillet heat oil and add chili powder. Stir and brown on low heat 1 minute.
2. Add eggs; season with salt. When the whites are set and edges cooked, add water.
3. Cover skillet and cook eggs to desired doneness.
4. (Serve with refried beans and hot flour tortillas.)
5. Serves 2-4.

HUEVO CON PEPINO SILVESTRE
(Egg and Gherkins Scramble)

8-10 wild gherkins, sliced thinly 1 tablespoon salt
2 tablespoons cooking oil ¼ teaspoon black pepper
3 eggs

1. In skillet heat oil and fry sliced gherkins. Stir and fry for 8-10 minutes.
2. Add eggs, salt, and black pepper to fried gherkins and stir egg to combine mixture.
3. Allow mixture to set on bottom and sides of pan. Stir lightly and cook 5 minutes or till eggs are cooked.
4. Serves 2-4.

HUEVOS RANCHEROS
(Spicy Ranch-Style Eggs)

¼ onion, chopped 3 large tomatoes, chopped
1 tablespoon cooking oil 2 large green chilies, seeded,
1 clove garlic   and chopped
1 teaspoon cumin and pepper- ½ teaspoon salt
corns, mixed 5-6 eggs

1. In skillet heat oil and saute onions.
2. Grind garlic and spices. Add water to make a paste. Add to onions.
3. Add chopped tomatoes, chilies, and salt to mixture and simmer for 10 minutes.
4. Eggs can now be cooked in this mixture by carefully breaking eggs into skillet one at a time.
5. When whites are set, cover skillet and cook eggs to desired doneness.
6. (Eggs may be prepared separately and then pour sauce over eggs.)
7. Serves 3-5. (Serve with flour tortillas.)

RIDDLE (ADIVINANZA)

Oro parece
plata no es
el que no lo acierte
bien bobo es.   (Plátano)

47

HUEVOS REVUELTOS CON SESOS
(Scrambled Eggs with Brains)

1½ cups brains, cooked	2 teaspoons salt
2 tablespoons butter	½ teaspoon black pepper
4 eggs	Cooking oil
2 tablespoons milk	

1. Cook brains in 1 quart water and ½ teaspoon salt. Simmer 10 minutes. Drain and cut in bite size pieces.
2. In skillet saute brains in butter.
3. Beat eggs, milk, salt, and pepper with fork.
4. Pour egg mixture over brains.
5. Stir mixture till it starts to set. Stir lightly and cook about 5 minutes till eggs are cooked but glossy and moist.
6. Serves 4-6. (Delicious with hot flour tortillas and *Ranchero* Sauce.)

HUEVOS REVUELTOS CON JAMÓN
(Scrambled Eggs with Ham)

1 tablespoon cooking oil	¼ cup milk
1 cup ham, cooked and cubed	2 teaspoons salt
4 eggs	¼ teaspoon black pepper

1. In skillet heat oil and brown cubed ham.
2. Beat eggs, milk, salt, and pepper with fork.
3. Pour egg mixture over ham.
4. Stir mixture till it starts to set. Stir lightly and cook 5 minutes or till eggs are cooked.
5. (May be used as a filling for *taquitos.*)
6. Serves 4-6.

RIDDLE (ADIVINANZA)

En el campo me crié,
metida entre verdes lazos;
aquél que llora por mí,
ése me hace mil pedazos.

(La cebolla)

HUEVOS REVUELTOS CON MIGAS
(Scrambled Eggs with Corn Tortilla Bits)

4 corn tortillas, broken up
  into bite-size pieces
½ garlic clove
1 teaspoon mixed spices
  (peppercorns and cumin)

4 eggs
2 teaspoons salt
¼ cup milk
2 tablespoons cooling oil

1. In skillet heat oil and fry bite-size tortillas till crisp.
2. Grind garlic and spices and add to fried chips. Stir and simmer 1 minute.
3. Beat eggs, milk, and salt.
4. Add egg mixture over chips. Stir mixture till it starts to set on bottom and sides of skillet. Stir lightly and cook until eggs are glossy and moist.
5. Serves 4-6.

MACHACADO
(Beef Jerky and Eggs)

¼ lb. beef jerky, chipped
2 tablespoons cooking oil
¼ cup onion, chopped
¼ cup green pepper, chopped
2 teaspoons salt

1 clove garlic
1 teaspoon mixed spices
  (peppercorns and cumin)
4 eggs

1. Boil jerky 15-20 minutes. Drain and cut up into small chips.
2. In skillet heat oil and saute chipped jerky, onion, and green pepper. (3 minutes)
3. Grind spices and garlic. Add to jerky, stir, and simmer for 1 minute.
4. Add eggs and salt to jerky and stir eggs to combine mixture.
5. Allow egg mixture to set. Stir lightly and cook until eggs are glossy but moist.
6. (Serve with hot flour tortillas and *Guacamole*.)
7. Serves 3-5.

PAPAS CON HUEVO
(Potato-Egg Scramble)

3	medium potatoes, peeled and diced	1 tablespoon salt
¼	cup cooking oil	1 teaspoon black pepper
6	slices bacon, cut in bite size pieces	¼ cup milk
		4 eggs

1. In skillet fry bacon till crisp. Remove bacon from skillet and drain on absorbent paper.
2. Add oil to bacon drippings in skillet and fry diced potatoes. (15-20 minutes).
3. Beat eggs, milk, salt and pepper.
4. Pour egg mixture over potatoes. Add crisp bacon bits.
5. Stir mixture till it starts to set. Stir lightly and cook till eggs are cooked glossy but moist.
6. (Serve as filling for *taquitos*.) Serves 4-6.

TOMATE VERDE CON HUEVO
(Green Tomato Scrambled with Egg)

2	large green tomatoes, chopped	¼ teaspoon black pepper
1	teaspoon cooking oil	2 eggs
		2 teaspoons salt

1. In skillet heat oil and fry green chopped tomatoes. Stir and fry for 5 minutes.
2. Add eggs, salt, and black pepper to fried tomatoes and stir eggs to combine mixture.
3. Allow mixture to set on bottom and sides of skillet. Stir lightly and cook until eggs are cooked.
4. Serves 2-4.

RIDDLE (ADIVINANZA)

Rita, Rita
Que en el monte grita
en la casa calladita

(El hacha)

TORTA A LA MEXICANA
(Mexican Omelet)

2	eggs	¼ teaspoon black pepper
2	tablespoons butter	1 large tomato
2	tablespoons milk	1 tablespoon green chili
1	teaspoon salt	pepper, diced
1	tablespoon onion, minced	

1. In small skillet saute onion, green chili peppers, and tomato in 1 tablespoon butter.
2. Beat eggs, milk, salt, and black pepper.
3. Heat an 8-inch skillet with flared sides. Add 1 tablespoon butter; tilt skillet to grease sides.
4. Pour in omelet mixture. Cook mixture slowly. Run spatula around edge, lifting to allow uncooked portion to flow underneath.
5. Spoon sauted mixture across center; fold sides of omelet over envelope-style, to hold in filling.
6. Tilt skillet and roll omelet onto hot plate. Serves 2.

TORTA DE HUEVO CON CHAMPIÑÓNES
(Mushroom Egg Omelet)

2	eggs	1 teaspoon salt
1	tablespoon butter	¼ teaspoon black pepper
2	tablespoons milk	¼ cup mushrooms, sliced and drained

1. Beat eggs, milk, salt, and black pepper.
2. In skillet melt butter and pour in egg mixture.
3. Cook mixture slowly. Run spatula around edge, lifting to allow uncooked portion to flow underneath.
4. Spoon mushrooms across center; fold sides of omelet over envelope-style, to hold in filling.
5. Tilt skillet and roll omelet onto hot plate. Serves 2.

ARROZ CON POLLO
(Rice-Chicken Skillet Dinner)

1	2½-3½ lbs. broiler fryer, cut up	1	8 oz. can tomato sauce
1	tablespoon salt	2	teaspoons mixed spices (cumin and peppercorns)
2	cups uncooked rice	2	cloves garlic
2	tablespoons cooking oil		boiling water

1. In a 4½ quart Dutch oven, brown chicken in 1 tablespoon oil. Add salt, cover and simmer 15-20 minutes.
2. Grind mixed spices and garlic. Add a little water and set aside.
3. In a skillet brown rice in 1 tablespoon oil.
4. Add browned rice to chicken. Cover and simmer 5 minutes.
5. Add spices, tomato sauce, and enough boiling water to cover. Simmer for 20-25 minutes.
6. Stir only once during the simmering process.
7. Serves 8-10. (Try the hot chili sauce with this dish.)
8. (Vermicelli could be substituted for rice.)

ENCHILADAS VERDES
(Green Enchiladas)

4	cups chicken breasts, cooked and cut finely	½ pint sour cream
	Oil for frying	4 cups Green Enchilada Sauce (page 26)
12	tortillas	

1. Lift tortillas, one at a time, with kitchen tongs and dip into ½" heated oil in skillet. (heat tortillas just for a few seconds; only long enough to soften)
2. Lift tortilla from oil, dip immediately into heated enchilada sauce.
3. Spoon about 1 tablespoon of shredded chicken into the center. Top with 2 teaspoons sour cream. Roll.
4. (Rolled enchiladas should be placed seamside down to keep filling in place.)
5. When all the tortillas have been stuffed, pour the remaining sauce over them and top with sour cream.
6. Bake for 15-20 minutes.
7. Serve at once. Serves 4-6.

ENVUELTOS DE POLLO
(Ranch Style Chicken Enchiladas)

1	2-3 lbs. broiler fryer, cooked and diced	2	cans whole tomatoes
6	cups water	1	clove garlic
1	tablespoon salt	1	teaspoon mixed spices
1	tablespoon cooking oil		(peppercorns and cumin)
½	small onion, diced	2	cups chicken broth
		12	corn tortillas

1. Boil cut up chicken in 6 cups water and salt. Simmer, covered, for 40-50 minutes. Reserve broth.
2. Remove bones from chicken. Dice chicken and set aside.
3. In skillet saute onion in oil.
4. Grind garlic and mixed spices, add a little water, and add to sautéed onions. Simmer for 1 minute.
5. Stir in whole tomatoes and broth. Simmer 5-10 minutes.
6. Dip tortillas one at a time in tomato mixture and place in casserole serving dish. Fill with chicken and roll like enchiladas. Place seam side down to keep filling in place.
7. Pour remaining sauce over envueltos. Bake in oven at 350_ for 10 minutes.
8. Serve hot. Serves 4-6.

POLLO EN MOLE
(Tasty Chicken Mole)

1	3-4 lbs. stewing chicken, cut up	¼	cup broth
1	cup fine dry cracker crumbs	1	tablespoon salt
	chicken broth	1	quart water
		1½	tablespoons prepared *Mole*

1. In a 4-quart Dutch oven combine chicken, water, and salt. Bring to boiling. Reduce heat; simmer, covered, for 30 minutes or till chicken is tender.
2. Drain chicken, but do reserve the broth.
3. Make a *mole* paste by mixing mole and ¼ cup broth. Add to chicken.
4. Add more broth to partially cover chicken.
5. Add fine dry cracker crumbs. Simmer 20 minutes, covered, stirring occasionally.
6. (Serve with rice.) Serves 6-8.

POLLO CON CALABAZA Y ELOTE
(Chicken with Squash and Corn)

1	2-3 lbs. fryer chicken, cut up	2	teaspoons mixed spices
3-4	tender Mexican squash, peeled and cubed	2	large fresh tomatoes, diced
1	tablespoon cooking oil	1	can whole kernel corn, drained
1	tablespoon salt	1	tablespoon flour
2	cloves garlic	⅓	cup water

1. Wash and cut off ends of squash, peel, and cut into cubes.
2. Grind mixed spices and garlic. Add a little water and set aside.
3. Brown cut-up chicken in oil. Add salt. Cover and simmer for 15-20 minutes.
4. Add squash cubes, spices, and diced tomatoes. Simmer for 30-40 minutes, covered stirring occasionally.
5. Add drained corn.
6. Mix 1 tablespoon flour and ⅓ cup water to make a paste. Add to mixture. Cook and stir until thickened and bubbly.
7. Serves 6-8.

POLLO EN SALSA
(Chicken in Spicy Tomato Sauce)

1	2-3 lbs. fryer, cut up	1	clove garlic
1	tablespoon salt	1½	teaspoon mixed spices (cumin and peppercorns)
1	tablespoon cooking oil		
1	6 oz. can tomato sauce	1	cup warm water
¼	cup green pepper, chopped	2	tablespoons flour—½ cup water

1. In a 4½ quart Dutch oven brown chicken in oil. Add salt, cover and simmer 15-20 minutes.
2. Grind mixed spices and garlic. Add a little water and set aside.
3. Add chopped green pepper, spices, and tomato sauce. Add water. Cover, simmer 25-35 minutes, stirring occasionally.
4. Mix 2 tablespoons flour and ½ cup water to make a paste. Add to mixture. Cook and stir till thickened and bubbly.
5. Serves 6-8.

TAMALES DE POLLO
(Chicken Tamales)

Masa for tamales:

4 cups masa (may be purchased at tortilla factory)	½ cup broth from cooked chicken filling mixture
1½ cups lard	2 tablespoons salt
2 red chili pods, boiled and sieved	

1. Slit chili pods to remove seed. Boil for 10 minutes. Drain.
2. Place masa in a large bowl, add lard and chili pods. Knead well.
3. Gradually add broth and salt. Knead well, using enough broth to make the mush spreadable.
4. Makes enough masa for 5 dozen tamales.

Chicken Filling for tamales:

2 tablespoons oil	3 teaspoons mixed spices (peppercorns and cumin)
8 cups chicken, cooked and diced	1 tablespoon salt
1 lb. corn shucks	3 cloves garlic
2 quarts boiling water	

1. Grind spices and garlic. Add a little water and sauté spices in oil for 1 minute.
2. Add diced cooked chicken, salt, and ½ cup water to spices.
3. Simmer for 5 minutes.
4. Combine ⅓ cup masa and ⅔ cup broth to make a paste. Add to thicken mixture.
5. Cook and stir till thickened and bubbly.
6. Soak corn shucks in one quart boiling water for 1 hour.
7. Drain shucks well.
8. Spread lower half (wider end) of each shuck with approximately 2 tablespoons of the masa, smoothing it over the surface of the shuck.
9. Spoon 2 tablespoons filling, lengthwise near the edge of the shuck.
10. Roll tamale jelly-roll fashion, starting at edge nearest filling. Fold over, small unfilled end of shuck, to seal in one end. Continue until all tamales are filled and rolled.

11. When ready to cook, cover the bottom of a large cooker with wet corn shucks (or use a large steamer with rack). Place a small heat proof bowl in the center of the cooker to keep the tamales in an upright position.
12. Arrange the tamales around the bottom of the cooker — folded end down — open end up. (This allows tamales to cook uniformly and retain their filling).
13. Cover tamales with damp cheese cloth or tea towel. Add one quart boiling water or enough to measure a depth of 3 inches.
14. Cover with lid and cook gently for 1 hour.
15. Make sure that liquid does not boil away. Add boiling water, if necessary, to prevent scorching.

TOSTADAS DE POLLO
(Rich Chicken-Filled Tostadas)

12	corn tortillas	1	cup American cheese, grated
	Oil for frying		
4	cups chicken, cooked and diced	2	cups lettuce, shredded
		2	cups tomatoes, diced
2	teaspoon salt	1	cup avocado dressing
½	teaspoon pepper		

1. Fry tortillas in a heavy skillet, one at a time, in about ½" hot oil. Lift tortilla with tongs and slide into hot oil. Fry until crisp but not tough. Turn once using tongs. Tostadas are left flat and not folded during or after frying.
2. Lift tortilla from oil and drain flat on a paper towel.
3. Place fried flat tortillas on a cookie sheet. Spoon grated cheese and cooked chicken (add salt and pepper to season diced chicken) on each tortilla.
4. Bake at 250° for 3-5 minutes. Allow cheese to melt.
5. Prepare avocado dressing by blending 2 avocados, 2 teaspoons garlic salt, and 1 cup sour cream.
6. Top *tostadas* with shredded lettuce, diced tomatoes, and avocado dressing.
7. (For beef *tostadas* substitute 4 cups cooked ground beef for diced cooked chicken.)

POLLO GUISADO
(Spicy Chicken and Gravy)

1 2-3 lbs. fryer, cut up	2 teaspoons mixed spices
1 tablespoon salt	(cumin and peppercorns)
1 tablespoon cooking oil	1 cup water
2 cloves garlic	2 tablespoons flour-
	2 cups water

1. Brown chicken in oil. Add salt, cover and simmer 15 minutes.
2. Grind mixed spices and garlic. Add a little water.
3. Add spices and 1 cup water. Cover, simmer 25-30 minutes, stirring occasionally.
4. Mix 2 tablespoons flour and 2 cups water to make a gravy. Add to mixture. Cook and stir till thickened and bubbly.
5. Serves 6-8.

RIDDLE (ADIVINANZA)

Alto, alto como un piño
Delgadito, delgadito como un comino

(El humo)

VERSITOS PARA ÑINOS
(Verses For Children)

El Gato y La Gata

El Gato y la Gata
se van a casar,
y el Gato no quiere
por no trabajar.

La Gallina

Vengan mis pollitos,
vamos a escarbar.
Dijo la gallina,
¡ Ca-ca-cara-cá!

La Mariposa

Mariposa luminosa,
Mariposa de puro oro,
en las alas un tesoro,
Mariposa voladora.

El Gusanito

Gusanito, gusantio,
teje, teje, sin cesar.
Teje ya tú capullito.
Téjelo hasta terminar.

El Día Que Tú Naciste

El día que tú naciste
nacieron las cosas bellas:
nació el sol, nació la luna
y nacieron las estrellas.

La Araña Pirulina

La araña Pirulina
por la pared se subió
y mi Tia Catalina
Con la escoba la barrió

Pin, Marin

Pin, Marín
de don Pingué
cúcara mácara
Pipirí fue.

Tortillitas

Tortillitas, tortillitas
tortillitas para papá
tortillitas para mamá
tortillitas de salvado
para papá cuando esta enojado;
tortillitas de manteca
para mamá que está contenta.

Que Se Le Quema

¡ Que se le quema a la niña
   la casa!
¡ Que se le quema!
¡ Que se le abrasa!
¡ Que se le quema la calabaza!

Madre Querida

Madre querida
eres mi amor.
Toma estas flores
del corazón.

Son las más bellas
de tu jardín
y hoy te cantamos
¡ Que seas feliz!

Huevo

Huevecito fresquecito
no te vayas a quebrar
proque a Lola y a Memito
los tendrás que alimentar.

Panes

(Breads)

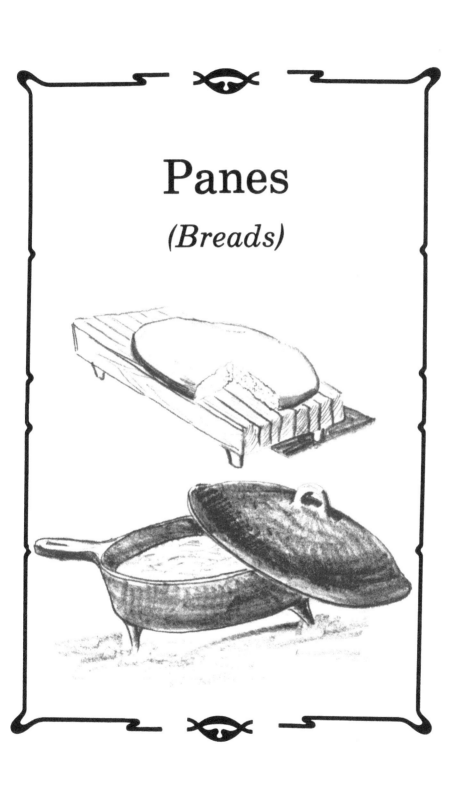

PAN DE CAMPO
(Camp Bread)

4	cups flour	1	teaspoon sugar
4	teaspoons double-action baking powder	¾	cup shortening
2	teaspoons salt	1½	cups milk

1. Preheat oven to 450°.
2. Mix all dry ingredients.
3. Blend in shortening with a pastry blender or rub it in with your fingertips.
4. Add just enough milk to make a smooth dough which can be handled without being too sticky.
5. Turn it out on a floured board and knead lightly (no more than one minute.)
6. Shape dough into large pattie or divide into two patties.
7. Roll out to ½" thick; place dough on a greased cookie sheet; prick all over dough pattie with a fork.
8. Bake at 450° for 12-15 minutes. (Delicious with *Carne Guisada*!)

Variations:

Skillet Camp Bread —

You may use a skillet if you are really roughing it and do not have an oven. Grease the skillet well. Pat out the dough to ¾" thick, and place it in the skillet. Put them over the grill or coals. Cover skillet with lid or heavy foil. Place hot coals over lid. Turn very carefully when bottom side is brown (6 minutes) and bake until the other side is brown (6 more minutes)

RIDDLE (ADIVINANZA)

Un águila
Muy feroz
Con el pico por delante
y los ojos por detrás

(Las tijeras)

60

PAN DE ELOTE
(Fresh Corn Coffeecake)

4 cups corn (4-6 ears of fresh corn)	4 tablespoons shortening 1 cup sugar

1. Remove husks and silk from corn. Cut corn from cobs.
2. Grind corn in blender.
3. In bowl, combine corn, sugar and shortening. Blend well.
4. Pour in a greased square pan and bake at 350° for 25-30 minutes or until golden brown.
5. Serve warm. (Excellent as a sweet treat for a coffee break.)
6. Serves 6-8.

PAN DE MAÍZ
(Easy Mexican Corn Bread)

1 cup cornmeal	2 teaspoons salt
1 cup American cheese, grated	2 eggs ½ cup cooking oil
1 8½ oz. can cream-style corn	1 teaspoon baking powder

1. Mix all ingredients in order listed.
2. Pour into baking dish or skillet.
3. Bake at 350° for 45 minutes. Serves 4-6.

PAN DE MAIZ CON JALAPEÑO
(Jalapeno Corn Bread)

2 eggs	1 cup milk or buttermilk
1 teaspoon salt	2 teaspoons baking powder
⅓ cup American cheese, grated	1 cup cornmeal
1 cup canned cream-style corn	3 or 4 jalapeno peppers, chopped
	¼ cup cooking oil

1. Mix all ingredients together.
2. Bake 1 hour at 350°.
3. (Serve with Savory Pinto Beans.)
4. Serves 6-8.

PUCHITAS DE ELOTE
(Fresh Corn Fritters)

3 cups corn (3-5 ears of fresh corn)	1 tablespoon flour
	1 cup cooking oil
½ cup sugar	1 tablespoon shortening

1. Remove husks and silk from corn. Cut corn from cobs.
2. Grind corn in blender.
3. In bowl, combine corn, sugar and shortening. Blend well.
4. Stir in flour.
5. Drop by tablespoonfuls in hot oil and allow each fritter to fry until golden brown. Drain on paper towels.
6. Makes 18-20 fritters. (Serve warm as a sweet snack.)

SOPAIPILLAS
(Hot Fried Puffs)

¼ cup warm water	⅓ cup sugar
1 pkg. yeast	1 teaspoon salt
1 egg	1 tablespoon cornmeal
1½ cup milk	5 cups flour
⅓ cup melted butter	

1. Mix warm water and yeast in electric blender, until thoroughly mixed.
2. Blend in remaining ingredients except 3 cups flour.
3. Put dough in large bowl. Cover and let stand in warm place about one hour.
4. Add remaining flour.
5. Knead into soft dough.
6. Cover, let rise until double in bulk.
7. Punch down and store in plastic bag in refrigerator.
8. Roll out thick. Cut triangularly or equilaterally.
9. Heat oil to 400°.
10. Fry until golden. Makes 8 dozen.
11. (Serve piping hot with butter and honey or sprinkle with sugar and cinnamon.)
12. (Dough may be kept in refrigerator for two weeks.)

TAMALES DE ELOTE
(Fresh Corn Tamales)

6   cups corn (10-12 ears of   3   cups boiling water
    fresh corn)   1½ tablespoons salt
    Fresh corn shucks   6   tablespoons shortening

1. Grind corn in blender.
2. Combine corn, salt, and shortening. Blend well.
3. Wrap 2 tablespoons of corn mixture in a fresh corn shuck.
4. Place tamales in a steaming pot by placing one layer vertically and one horizontally.
5. Pour boiling water over them and cook 1 hour.
6. Makes 4 dozen.
7. (Serve as a hot bread with pinto beans and fresh tomato slices.)

TAMALES DULCES DE ELOTE
(Sweet Corn Tamales)

6   cups corn (10-12 ears   3   cups boiling water
    of fresh corn)   Fresh corn shucks
1½ cups sugar   6   tablespoons shortening

1. Remove shucks and silk from corn. Reserve shucks.
2. Cut corn from cobs.
3. Grind corn in blender.
4. In large bowl, combine corn, sugar, and shortening. Blend well.
5. Wrap 2 tablespoons of mixture in a fresh corn shuck.
6. Place tamales in a steaming pot by placing each layer in a crisscross fashion (one layer vertically and one horizontally.)
7. Pour boiling water and cook 1 hour.
8. Serve hot. (A delicious sweet snack served with cold milk.)
9. Makes 4 dozen.

TORTILLAS DE HARINA
(Flour Tortillas)

4 cups flour	1 teaspoon baking powder
⅔ cup shortening	hot water (1 cup approx.)
2 teaspoons salt	

1. Mix all dry ingredients.
2. Blend shortening with pastry blender or fingers.
3. Pour hot water and mix to a thick dough. (water must be poured all at once.)
4. Knead on a bread board until soft and pliable. Allow dough to stand for 20 minutes.
5. Preheat ungreased griddle.
6. Make dough balls (size of a golf ball) and form into flat patties.
7. Roll out on bread board until the patty is round and thin.
8. Bake on preheated griddle. Turn tortillas when top side begins to show some puffiness or blisters. Turn to other side.
9. Cook other side until lightly brown. Place in bread basket and keep covered.
10. (To prepare *taquitos*, use cooked flour tortillas. Spoon heated filling in center of warm tortilla and fold jelly-roll style.)

TORTILLAS DE MANTECA
(Short Corn Tortillas)

2 cups fresh masa (purchase at tortilla factory)	1 cup pure lard
2 teaspoons salt	½ cup cracklings

1. Combine first 3 ingredients and blend well with hand.
2. Add cracklings and blend again.
3. Divide dough into 8-10 balls (golf size)
4. Pat out small flat circles and place on ungreased griddle.
5. Tortillas begin to fry in their own grease. Allow each side to fry to a golden brown. Drain on absorbent paper.
6. Serve warm as a hot bread. Serves 6-8.

TORTILLAS DE MASA
(Corn Tortillas)

2 cups Masa Harina	2 tablespoons margarine
1 teaspoon salt	1¼ cup warm water

1. Mix masa harina and salt. Add margarine.
2. Add warm water all at once and use fingers to work mixture into a soft dough.
3. Knead dough until no longer sticky.
4. Divide dough into 12-16 balls; cover and let dough rest 20 minutes at room temperature.
5. Place a small square of wax paper on the bottom part of open tortilla press. Place a ball almost on the center of the wax paper. (a little more towards the hinge of the press than the handle.)
6. Place a second wax paper square, well flattened, on top of the ball. Close the press down firmly until the tortilla measures about 6" in diameter.
7. Peel the top wax paper off the dough. Pick up the second wax paper square and place the flattened dough onto the palm of your hand. Then peel off the wax paper and place the tortilla onto a moderately hot griddle.
8. In a few seconds the edges of the tortilla will begin to dry out, at this point, turn the tortilla.
9. Allow the second side to cook for a slightly longer period until it is slightly browned.
10. Flip it back onto the first side and let it finish cooking. Allow 2 minutes cooking time per tortilla.
11. (Delicious served with any Mexican dish.) Serves 6-8.

RIDDLE (ADIVINANZA)

Hay una cosa muy clara
que al decir "te la digo"
es nombrarla.
Y sin embargo te la digo
y no lo entiendes.

(Tela)

VERSITOS PARA ÑINOS
(Verses For Children)

Bandera

Banderita de mi Pátria
Banderita de mi amor
te prometo ser valiente
y defenderte con honor.

Arbol

El árbol frondoso
muy lindo se ve
con manzanas rojas
y el tronco café.

Un Pájarito

¿ Qué tienes alli?
Un pájarito —
¿ Con qué lo mantienes?
Con pan y quesito
¿ Lo mataremos? —
¡ Hay, no pobrecito!

Tengo, Tengo, Tengo

Tengo, tengo, tengo
Tu no tienes nada
Tengo tres ovejas,
En mi manada
Una me da leche
Y otra mantequilla
Para la semana.

Mi Amigo Martín

Yo tengo un amigo
que se llama Martín
Que brinca y que
salta como un chapulín

Mi Carita

Una boquita para comer,
Una naracita para oler,
Dos ojitos para ver,
Dos oídos para oír,
Y la cabecita para dormir.

Tíos Y Primos

Mi mamá tiene un hermano
Que me tío viene a ser
Y tiene dos hermanitas
Que mis tías son también
Los hijitos de mis tíos
Mis primos hermanos son
Y por ser de mi familia
A todos los quiero yo.

Patito, Patito

Patito, patito
color de café
Si usté no me quiere
Pues luego, ¿ Por que?
Ya no se presuma
Que al cabo yo sé
Que usté es un patito
Color de café.

Me dijo que sí
Ya luego que no;
Era una patita
Como todas son.

La pata voló
Y el pato también;
Y nunca jamás
A los dos encontré.
(Repeat entire song.)

Postres

(Desserts)

ATOLE DE ARROZ
(Rice Pudding)

3 cups milk	½ cup raisins
⅔ cup rice, uncooked	1 teaspoon cinnamon
¾ cup sugar	

1. In a saucepan, combine milk and rice. Cook 15 minutes over medium heat.
2. Add sugar, cinnamon, and raisins. Cover and cook 15-20 minutes.
3. Serve warm. Serves 4-6.

ATOLE PINOLE
(Roasted Cornmeal Pudding)

½ cup pinole (roasted corn-meal mix)	½ cup sugar
	½ cup water
3 cups milk	

1. In saucepan, heat milk over low heat.
2. Mix pinole, sugar, and water to make a paste.
3. Pour pinole paste into milk and cook until mixture thickens, about 10 minutes.
4. Serve it thick and eat with a spoon.

RIDDLE (ADIVINANZA)

Blanco por fuera,
negro por dentro
y por una puenta
le pegan el fuego.

(El cigarro)

BUÑUELOS
(Fried Cinnamon Crisps)

4 cups flour	¼ cup shortening
¼ teaspoon salt	1 egg, beaten
1½ tablespoons sugar	1 cup anise tea

1. Prepare one cup tea by boiling 3 teaspoons anise.
2. Sift dry ingredients and add shortening and blend.
3. Add beaten egg and lukewarm tea to dry ingredients and knead dough.
4. Make small dough balls and shape into patties. Let stand for one hour.
5. Roll out as thin as possible.
6. Fry in deep fat until golden brown. (Prick tortillas with a fork when dropped into hot fat to make them puff.)
7. In brown paper bag mix 4 teaspoons ground stick cinnamon to 4 tablespoons sugar. Toss fried crisp tortilla in paper bag to coat with cinnamon-sugar mixture.
8. (Popular New Year's Eve dessert served with hot cocoa.)

CAPIROTADA
(Bread Pudding)

5 cups water	18 slices of bread
2 cinnamon sticks	12 slices of cheese
3 thin slices of onion	1 cup raisins
2 cups sugar	1 apple, thinly sliced
1 tablespoon shortening	

1. Brew tea with first 5 ingredients. Strain.
2. Line square casserole dish with six slices bread.
3. Top with a slice of cheese on each slice of bread, sprinkle with raisins and thinly sliced apple. Add tea to soak layer.
4. Repeat layers bread — cheese — raisins — apples and tea.
5. Top with bread only for last layer. Add remaining tea to soak thoroughly.
6. Bake at 350° for 25-30 minutes until golden brown.
7. Serve warm or cold. (A favorite Lenten dessert or snack.)

COCHINITOS
(Gingerbread Piglets)

3½ cups flour, sifted	½ cup margarine
1 teaspoon ginger	½ cup sugar
1 teaspoon cinnamon	1 egg
¼ teaspoon cloves	¾ cup light molasses
½ teaspoon salt	1 cup buttermilk
1 teaspoon soda	

1. Sift flour, spices, soda, and salt together. Set aside.
2. Cream margarine, sugar, and egg on medium speed for 2 minutes.
3. Beat in molasses on medium speed for 1 minute.
4. Blend in dry ingredients and buttermilk alternately.
5. Roll on well floured board into ¼ inch thick. Cut with pig shaped cookie cutter.
6. Bake on ungreased cookie sheets at 375° for 6-8 minutes.

DULCE DE CALABAZA
(Pumpkin Candy)

1 large pumpkin, ripe	water
lime (cae)	sugar

1. Cut pumpkin into uniform wedges or slices.
2. Peel and cut pieces of desired size.
3. Soak overnight in lime water to cover. (Use 1 tablespoon lime to each quart of water. Stir lime water well before pouring over pumpkin.)
4. Remove pumpkin from lime water and wash thoroughly, three or more times in clear water.
5. Cover pumpkin with warm water and bring slowly to boiling point. Boil for 5 minutes.
6. Drain and wash twice in clear cold water. Drain for an hour.
7. Pierce each piece in several places with a fork so that sugar syrup can be absorbed.
8. Weigh pumpkin and use equal amount of sugar.
9. Cover pumpkin with sugar, moisten with water and bake at 300° until pumpkin is crystallized. (about 3 hours)
10. Drain and place pumpkin on wax paper to dry.

DULCE DE LECHE
(Pecan Pralines)

1 cup brown sugar	2 cups pecans
1 cup granulated sugar	½ cup evaporated milk

1. Mix all ingredients thoroughly.
2. Cook over medium heat to softball stage, stirring constantly.
3. Beat until mixture starts to thicken.
4. Drop candy rapidly from a spoon on to buttered wax paper to form patties.
5. (If candy becomes too stiff, stir in a little hot water to make it smooth.)

EMPANADAS DE CALABAZA
(Baked Pumpkin Foldover)

Filling:	Dough:
4 cups pumpkin, cooked	3 cups flour
2 cups sugar	1½ teaspoons salt
1 stick cinnamon	1 cup shortening
2 teaspoons cinnamon	12 tablespoons beer
½ teaspoon nutmeg	
½ teaspoon ginger	

1. Combine all ingredients and cook until thick and caramelized. (about 1 hour.)

Dough:

1. Combine flour and salt.
2. Cut in shortening with pastry blender.
3. Make well in center and add beer all at once.
4. Stir with a fork until mixture becomes dough.
5. Shape dough into dough ball. Pinch off small amounts of dough and shape into small round patties. (Allow patties to stand about 30 minutes.)
6. Roll out on a lightly floured board and spoon pumpkin mixture into round; fold over and seal edges together by pressing with a fork.
7. Prick top of foldover to allow steam to escape.
8. Place foldovers on a cookie sheet and bake at 350° for 15-20 minutes.

71

EMPANADAS DE MANZANA
(Apple Foldovers)

Filling:	Dough:
4 cups apples, diced	3 cups flour
1½ cups sugar	1½ teaspoon salt
1 teaspoon cinnamon	1 cup shortening
¼ teaspoon nutmeg	12 tablespoons water
1 tablespoon cornstarch	
1 tablespoon lemon juice	
3 tablespoons butter	

1. Combine all ingredients and cook until apples are tender and mixture is thick. (about 1 hour)

Dough:

1. Combine flour and salt.
2. Cut in shortening with pastry blender.
3. Make well in center and add water all at once.
4. Stir with fork until mixture becomes dough.
5. Press together to form dough. Pinch off small amounts of dough and shape into small round patties.
6. Roll out on a lightly floured board and spoon apple filling into round; fold over and seal edges by pressing with fork tines. Prick top of foldovers to allow steam to escape.
7. Place foldovers on a cookie sheet and bake at 350° for 15-20 minutes.

RIDDLE (ADIVINANZA)

Me salen de la boca
nadie las puede ver
pero con ellas puedo
hacerme yo entender

(las palabras)

FLAN
(Custard with Caramel Sauce)

4 eggs	¼ cup sugar
2 cups milk	2 teaspoons vanilla

1. Beat eggs until smooth.
2. Add remaining ingredients and beat until smooth.
3. Pour mixture into well buttered custard cups.
4. Place cups in a large pan, which has been filled with just enough hot water to come up around baking custard cups.
5. Bake at 350° for 1 hour, or until a knife inserted in center comes out clean.
6. Chill for several hours before serving.
7. Spread an even thin layer of lump-free light brown sugar on top of already cooked and chilled custard.
8. Place under broiler, until sugar is partially melted and lightly browned. Serve at once.
9. Serves 6-8.

FRITAS
(Fried Sweet Puffs)

2 cups flour	3 tablespoons shortening
1 tablespoon sugar	1 egg, beaten
1 teaspoon baking powder	½ cup anise tea

1. Prepare ½ cup tea by boiling 1 teaspoon anise seed and 1 cup water. Strain tea.
2. Sift dry ingredients and add shortening and blend.
3. Add beaten egg and lukewarm tea to dry ingredients and knead into dough.
4. Make dough balls (size of golf balls) and shape into flat patties. Allow dough to stand 10-15 minutes.
5. Roll out tortilla and cut in fourths.
6. Drop in deep fat and prick with fork so that puffs will puff. Fry until golden brown.
7. Drain on absorbent paper and sprinkle with cinnamon and sugar mixture (½ cup sugar and 2 teaspoons cinnamon)

JALEA DE TOMATE
(Tomato Preserve)

6 lbs. tomatoes   3-6 cloves, whole
5 cups sugar   1 bottle fruit pectin
2 sticks cinnamon

1. Blanch and peel tomatoes.
2. Cut up in chunks and place in large cooking pot.
3. Add cinnamon sticks, cloves, and sugar. Cook to boil until mixture loses moisture content. (1-2 hours)
4. Add fruit pectin and cook until thick and pasty. (30 minutes).
5. Fill prepared jelly jars.

JALEA DE TUNA
(Cactus Fruit Jelly)

6 cups ripe cactus fruit   1½ cups water
  (*tunas*)

1. Cut ripe cactus fruit off prickly pear cactus.
2. Peel fruit and cut into small pieces
3. Add fruit to 1½ cups water and boil until soft. (20-30 minutes).
4. Drain through strainer, pressing to get all the juice. (3½ cups.)

For Jelly:

3½ cups cactus fruit juice   7 cups sugar
¼ cup lemon juice   1 bottle fruit pectin

1. In large pot mix juice, sugar, and lemon juice and bring to a hard rolling boil.
2. Add bottle of fruit pectin and bring to a rolling boil again.
3. Boil one minute, remove from heat, skim off foam.
4. Pour in prepared jars and seal with paraffin.

TORTILLAS DE AZÚCAR
(Sweet Tea Tortillas)

2 cups flour
⅔ cup shortening
¾ cup sugar

1 teaspoon baking powder
1 cup anise tea

1. Mix dry ingredients.
2. Blend shortening with pastry blender or fingers.
3. Boil one and a half cup water and add 3 teaspoons anise seed. Strain.
4. Pour hot tea and mix to a thick dough.
5. Make dough balls (size of golf balls) and shape into flat patties.
6. Roll out with rolling pin.
7. Bake on preheated griddle. Allow each side to cook 2 minutes. (Tortillas should be crisp and lightly brown.)
8. Serve with hot tea or coffee.

PAN DE POLVO
(Mexican Wedding Cookies)

2½ lbs. flour (10 cups)
2 lbs. vegetable shortening
   (3½ cups)

1 cup sugar
3 sticks cinnamon

1. Blend sugar and cinnamon in blender till cinnamon is finely ground.
2. Sift flour, sugar, and cinnamon.
3. Work shortening until dough is formed. (the heat of the hands will eventually make it into a soft pliable dough)
4. Let dough stand for 1 hour.
5. Roll out the dough and cut with tiny cookie cutters. (if large cookie shapes are used cookies will break and crumble.)
6. Bake at 375° for 5-7 minutes.
7. Roll in cinnamon and sugar. (Use 4 teaspoons ground stick cinnamon to 4 tablespoons sugar.)

MOLLETES
(Favorite Mexican Sweet Bread)

Topping mixture:

⅔ cup flour	¼ cup margarine
2 egg yolks, beaten	½ cup sugar

1. In bowl combine all first 3 ingredients.
2. Cut in margarine until mixture resembles fine crumbs.
3. With fork stir in egg yolks.
4. Mix with hands till well blended.
5. Divide dough into 15 balls.
6. On lightly floured surface roll each ball to a 3-inch circle. Set aside.

Dough:

4 cups flour	¼ cup shortening
1 pkg. active dry yeast	1 teaspoon salt
1 cup milk	2 eggs
¼ cup sugar	

1. In large bowl combine 2 cups of the flour and yeast.
2. In saucepan heat milk, sugar, shortening, and salt just till warm, shortening should almost begin to melt.
3. Add to dry mixture in bowl; add eggs.
4. Beat at low speed with electric mixer for ½ minute. Beat 3 minutes at high speed.
5. Stir in enough of the remaining flour to make a stiff dough. This step is done by hand.
6. Place on a lightly floured surface; knead till smooth. (10 minutes) Shape into a ball. Place in greased bowl, turning once to grease surface.
7. Cover; let rise till double. (1-1½ hours.) Punch down.
8. Divide into 15 smooth balls.
9. On lightly floured surface roll each piece to a 3-inch circle.
10. Place 2 inches apart on a greased baking sheet.
11. With spatula transfer topping circles to circles of dough on baking sheet.
12. Slash tops with a crisscross pattern. Cover; let rise till double, about 30 minutes.
13. Bake 375° for 15 minutes.

PAN DE LEVADURA
(Sweet Mexican Yeast Bread)

1 pkg. active dry yeast	1 teaspoon salt
¼ cup warm water	1 egg
¾ cup lukewarm milk	¼ cup shortening
1 teaspoon anise seed	3¾-4 cups flour
¾ cup sugar	

1. In mixing bowl, dissolve yeast in warm water.
2. Add milk, sugar, anise, salt, egg, shortening, and half of the flour. Mix with spoon until smooth.
3. Add enough remaining flour to handle easily; mix with hand.
4. Turn onto lightly floured board; knead until smooth and elastic (5 minutes). Place greased side up in greased bowl.
5. Cover; let rise in warm place until double. (about 1½ hours.)
6. Punch down; let rise again almost double. (about 30 minutes.)
7. Shape into braids. (Pinch small amounts of dough and make strips by shaping dough into strips; hold one end of strip in one hand and twist other end, until two ends are brought together. (makes a braid-like twist)
8. Cover and let rise until double in size. (15-20 minutes)
9. Bake at 400° for 12-15 minutes in lightly greased pan.
10. Serve hot. Make 2 dozen rolls.

SOPA DE PAN
(Bread Pudding)

6 cups firm white bread, diced	1 cup American cheese, diced
½ cup melted margarine	½ cup raisins
1 teaspoon cinnamon	2 cups milk
1 cup sugar	

1. In a large mixing bowl, combine all ingredients.
2. Pour mixture into a buttered oblong pan.
3. Bake at 350° for 30 minutes.
4. Spoon warm into serving dishes, or allow to cool and cut in squares. (It is delicious served warm or cold.)

SEMITAS
(Anise Seed Buns)

4 cups flour	¼ cup shortening
1 pkg. active dry yeast	1 teaspoon salt
1 cup anise tea	2 eggs
¼ cup sugar	

1. In large bowl combine 2 cups of the flour and the yeast.
2. In saucepan prepare anise tea by boiling 1½ cup water and 3 teaspoons anise. Add sugar, shortening, and salt to tea. When tea mixture is lukewarm, add to dry ingredients. (Do not strain tea, the anise seeds go into the dough.)
3. Add eggs. Beat at low speed for ½ minute. Beat 3 minutes at high speed.
4. Stir in enough of the remaining flour and knead to make a stiff dough.
5. Turn out onto a lightly floured surface; knead till smooth (10 minutes).
6. Shape into a ball. Place in greased bowl turn once to grease surface. Cover; let rise 1 hour.
7. Punch down. Divide dough into 10-15 pieces; shape each into a small ball.
8. On lightly floured surface roll or pat each piece to a 3-inch circle. Place 2 inches apart on a greased baking sheet.
9. Cover; let rise 30 minutes.
10. Bake at 375° for 18 minutes.

LECHE QUEMADA
(Burnt Milk Candy)

1¼ lbs. sugar (2½ cups)	¼ cup water
3 cups milk	1 cup pecan halves
1 tablespoon butter	

1. In large saucepan combine sugar and water.
2. Set over low heat; stir constantly. (Do not allow to scorch.)
3. When syrup will spin from the spoon (hardcrack), add butter and add milk gradually.
4. Boil until thick, stirring constantly until softball stage. Remove from heat.
5. Beat 20 minutes. Spread on a buttered square pan. Top with pecan halves; cool and cut into squares.

Puerco

(Pork)

CARNE DE PUERCO CON CALABAZA
(Pork-Squash Skillet Dinner)

1½ lbs. pork loin, cubed	2 cloves garlic
3-4 Mexican squash, peeled and cubed	1½ teaspoon mixed spices (peppercorns and cumin)
1 tablespoon cooking oil	1 tablespoon flour
1 tablespoon salt	⅓ cup water

1. Wash and cut off ends of squash, peel, and cut into cubes.
2. Grind mixed spices and garlic. Add a little water and set aside.
3. Brown cubed meat in oil. Add salt. Cover and simmer for 15 minutes.
4. Add squash cubes, and spices. Simmer for 30 minutes; covered, stirring occasionally.
5. Mix 1 tablespoon flour and ⅓ cup water to make a paste to thicken mixture. Add to squash mixture, stir, and cover.
6. Simmer for 10 minutes until mixture thickens.
7. Serves 6-8.

CHORIZO
(Mexican Pork Sausage)

5 lbs. pork roast, ground coarse	5 teaspoons cumin and peppercorns, mixed
2 cups white vinegar	3 tablespoons salt
5 large chili pods, rinsed, seeded, and softened in hot water	10 cloves garlic
	20 feet pork sausage casings

1. In blender combine vinegar, chili pods, garlic, cumin and pepper. Cover; blend till spices all ground.
2. Grind pork meat with coarse blade of food grinder.
3. Add seasoning mixture to meat and grind again.
4. Attach sausage stuffer attachment to grinder. Using a 3-4 feet piece of casing at a time, push casing onto stuffer, allow some to extend beyond end of attachment.
5. Grind mixture together, allowing it to fill casing. Fill casing till firm, but not overly full.
6. Tie with string or twist casing when links are 4-5 inches long. Casing may be omitted if desired. Wrap links in foil.
7. Wrap and refrigerate for three days. Wrap, label, and freeze.

CHULETAS DE PUERCO RANCHERAS
(Ranch-Style Pork Chops)

4-6 pork chops, ½" thick	4 large tomatoes, diced
1 tablespoon cooking oil	1 clove garlic
1 tablespoon salt	1 teaspoon mixed spices (peppercorns and cumin)
¼ onion, minced	
¼ cup water	

1. Grind garlic and mixed spices. Add a little water and set aside.
2. Brown pork chops in oil. Add salt. Cover and simmer for 10-15 minutes.
3. Add diced tomatoes, chopped onion, spices, and water. Simmer for 20 minutes; covered, stirring occasionally.
4. Serves 4-6.

GUISADO DE PUERCO
(Savory Mexican Pork Dish)

3-4 lb. pork meat or ribs, cubed
or cut in riblets
1 tablespoon cooking oil
1 tablespoon salt
1 teaspoon mixed spices
(cumin and peppercorns)

1 tablespoon flour
1 tablespoon oil
1 clove garlic
3 large chili pods

1. Slit chilies to remove seeds. Boil for 10 minutes just enough to tenderize. Drain.
2. Cut pork meat into small cubes and if using ribs cut into individual riblets. Both may be combined.
3. Brown cubed meat and riblets in 1 tablespoon oil. Add salt. Cover.
4. Grind garlic, spices, and chili pods. Add a little water and set aside.
5. In small skillet brown flour in 1 tablespoon oil and add spices. Stir and simmer for 2 minutes. Add this mixture to browned meat.
6. Simmer for 25 minutes; covered, stirring occasionally.
7. Serves 6-8.

PUERCO EN MOLE
(Pork-Mole Main Dish)

3-4 lbs. pork loin, cubed chunks
1 tablespoon cooking oil
2 teaspoons salt
1 quart water
Broth

1½ tablespoons prepared *Mole*
1½ cup fine dry cracker crumbs

1. In large pot brown cubed pork. Add salt, and water. Cook over medium heat 20-30 minutes. Drain, but do reserve the broth.
2. Make a *mole* paste by mixing 1½ tablespoons *mole* and ¼ cup broth. Add to pork.
3. Add more broth to partially cover pork.
4. Add fine dry cracker crumbs. Simmer 20 minutes; covered, stirring occasionally.
5. Serves 8-10.

PUERCO HORNADO EN ADOBE
(Marinated Roast Pork Ole)

4	lbs. pork roast	2	teaspoon mixed spices
1	tablespoon salt		(peppercorns and cumin)
2	clove garlic	2	chili pods

1. Slit chili pods and remove seeds. Boil in water for 10 minutes to tenderize.
2. Grind garlic, spices, and chili pods. Add a little water and set aside for basting.
3. Baste pork roast thoroughly with chili paste and salt.
4. Wrap roast with foil. Bake at 300° for 1 hour.
5. Serves 8-10.

REPOLLO CON CARNE DE PUERCO
(Favorite Cabbage-Pork Dinner)

1	cabbage, cut in eight chunks	2	cloves garlic
1½	lbs. pork loin, cubed	1	teaspoons mixed spices (peppercorns and cumin)
1	tablespoon cooking oil	1	large tomato, diced
1	teaspoon salt		

1. Grind garlic and mixed spices. Add a little water and set aside.
2. Rinse cabbage, cut in half, quarters, and then in eighths.
3. Brown cubed meat in oil. Add salt. Simmer for 20 minutes.
4. Add cabbage, spices, and diced tomato. Simmer for 20-30 minutes. Cover and stir occasionally.
5. (Do not add liquid. The flavor of this dish is enhanced by the fact that no liquid is used other than that which exudes from the ingredients.)
6. Serves 6-8.

TAMALES DE PUERCO
(Savory Pork Tamales)

Masa for Tamales:

4	cups masa (can be pur-chased at a tortilla factory)	½	cup broth, from the cooked meat mixture
1½ cups lard		2	tablespoons salt
2	red chili pods, boiled		

1. Slit chilies to remove seeds. Boil for 10 minutes just enough to tenderize chili pods. Drain.
2. Place masa in large mixing bowl, add lard and chili pods. Knead well.
3. Makes enough masa for 5 dozen tamales.

Pork filling for Tamales:

3	tablespoons cooking oil	3-4	dried red chili pods
3	lbs. pork, coarsely ground	3	cloves garlic
1	tablespoon salt	3	teaspoons mixed spices
1	pound corn shucks		(peppercorns and cumin)
2	quarts boiling water		

1. Slit chili pods to remove seeds. Boil for 10 minutes to tenderize pods. Drain.
2. Grind garlic, mixed spices, and chili pods. Add a little water.
3. Cook meat in oil until brown, add spices and one cup water. Simmer, uncovered for 20 minutes.
4. Combine ⅓ cup masa and ⅔ cup broth (from meat mixture) to make a paste. Add to thicken mixture.
5. Cook and stir till thickened and bubbly.
6. Soak corn shucks in one quart boiling water for 1 hour.
7. Drain shucks well.
8. Spread lower half (wider end) of each shuck with approximately 2 tablespoons of the masa, smoothing it over the surface of the shuck.
9. Spoon 2 tablespoons of the meat filling, lengthwise near the edge of the shuck.
10. Roll tamale jelly-roll fashion, starting at edge nearest filling. Fold over, small unfilled end of shuck, to seal in one end. Continue until all tamales are filled and rolled.

11. When ready to cook, cover the bottom of a large cooker with wet corn shucks (or use a large steamer with rack). Place a small heat-proof bowl in the center of the cooker to keep the tamales in an upright position.
12. Arrange the tamales around the bottom of the cooker — folded end down — open up. (this allows tamales to cook uniformly and retain their fillings.
13. Cover tamales with damp cheesecloth or tea towel. Add one quart boiling water or enough to measure a depth of 3 inches.
14. Cover with lid and cook gently for 1 hour and 15 minutes.
15. Make sure that liquid does not boil away. Add water, if necessary, to prevent scorching.
16. To reheat tamales, place in oven at 300° for 20 minutes or over a griddle 15 minutes, turning occasionally.

RIDDLE (ADIVINANZA)

Lo vemos, en lo alto,
de dia, muy azul;
mas usa en las noches
un negro capuz.

(el cielo)

GLOSSARY

Chile colorado: This chili is also referred to as *chile ancho.* This chili is sold as dried chili pods. It is a very popular ingredient in Mexican cookery. These pods have to be rinsed, seeded, and boiled for 15 minutes to soften before using.

Chile dulce: This is our bell pepper or also known as *chile verde.* This type of chili is also used for baked *Chile Rellenos,* and is usually used in numerous Mexican dishes along with onions and tomatoes.

Chilipetin: A small green chili (fresh) or red (dried), and it grows wild in South Texas country side. Most Mexican families have this pepper plant in their backyards. This chili is best for chili sauces.

Cilantro: Coriander and is usually sold fresh in stores. This is a must for the *Frijoles A La Mexicana.* To keep fresh place *cilantro* bunch in a water-filled glass in the refrigerator. It keeps for about one week. It is easily found in the fresh produce section of a supermarket.

Chiles verdes: These peppers are used traditionally in *Chiles Rellenos.* They are long and slender, fairly mild, smooth skinned and green.

Jalapeño: These chilies are smooth skinned, green, and very hot. They are usually sold in cans, sliced or whole and pickled in *escabeche,* spiced vinegar.

Masa: This is freshly ground daily at tortilla factories. Corn is soaked in lime water and then cooked and rinsed before grinding. Lime aids as a preservative and adds color. Fresh *masa* is best for *tamales* and corn tortillas, but instant *masa* is also available.

Panza: The large intestine of the cow which holds the cud. This is what is cleansed and used for *menudo.*

Taquitos: These roll-ups are most delicious and a favorite. *Taquitos* consist of flour tortillas plus any type of tasty meat or egg filling. *Chorizo con Huevo, Papas con Huevo, Frijoles Refritos,* and *Carne Guisada* are the most popular fillings.

Tomatillo: These are small green, piquant tomatoes. They are usually sold canned, and fresh in fruit stands and stores when in season. This is the main ingredient for *Enchiladas Verdes.*

Tortilla press: A cast iron press for pressing corn tortillas into flat thin circles. These can be purchased in most fruit stands and grocery stores in this area. This invention enables the homemaker to make her tortillas with ease and perfection. *Tamales* are also spread with this press.

Tripas de cabrito: The small intestines of a young kid goat. These tripes are cleansed thoroughly and used for wrapping *machitos.*

Tripas de res: Beef tripes or small intestines which are cleansed thoroughly and cooked on the grill, *Tripas Asadas. Tripas* are usually prepared to eat as appetizers during the cook-out or until the meat is ready to serve.

RIDDLE (ADIVINANZA)

Sigo a la Tarde
y llego contenta,
trayendo sombras,
luna y estrellas.

(la noche)

87

VERSITOS PARA ÑINOS
(Verses For Children)

Los Elefantitos

Cinco elefantitos,
Este *se cayo*
Cuatro elefantitos,
Este *se perdio,*
Tres elefantitos,
Este *se enfermo*
Dos elefantitos,
Este *se murio*
Y ahora quedo uno,
Solo *se quedo*
Este elefantito,
Me lo llevo yo,
Me lo llevo yo.

El Ro, Ro

A la ro, ro niño,
a la ro, ro, ro,
cierra tus ojitos
ciérralos, mi amor.

Duérmete, min niño,
que yo estoy aqui,
y los angelitos
cuidarán de ti.

Al mismo tiempo que se recitan estas rimas, se dan palmadas de una mano con la otra.

Tortillitas de Manteca

Tortillitas de Manteca
Pa' mamá que esta contenta;
Tortillitas de salvado
Pa' papá que está enojado.

Tortillitas de Papá

Una bolita de masa
Le pedí a mi mamá
Quiero hacer las tortillitas
Para darle a mi papá

Tortillitas muy redondas
Que le gustan a papá
Si las hago muy bonitas
Todas se las comerá

Tortillitas

¡ Tortillitas 'pa mamá
Las quemadas pa papá!

Otras rimas:

Los Pollitos

Cinco pollitos tiene me tía,
Uno le salta, otro le pía
Y otro le canta la sinfonía.

Andrés Méndez García

Pon, Pon

Pon, Pon
El dedito en el pilón
Acetón a la mesita
¡ ay, ay, ay, mi cabecita!

Los Cochinitos

Este compró un huevo,
Este encendió el fuego,
Esta trajo la sal,
Este lo guisó,
¡ Y este pícaro gordo se lo comió!